Never In Your Wildest DREAMS

A Transformational Story to Tap Into Your Hidden Gifts to
Create a Life of Passion, Purpose and Prosperity.

Natalie Ledwell

SHERPA
PRESS

Never in Your Wildest Dreams
A Transformational Story to Tap Into Your Hidden Gifts
to Create a Life of Passion, Purpose and Prosperity.

Sherpa Press
1621 Central Avenue
Cheyenne, WY 82001

Sherpa Press books may be purchased for educational, business, or sales promotional use. For information, please write:
Special Markets
Sherpa Press
1621 Central Avenue
Cheyenne, WY 82001

First Edition

Library of Congress Cataloging-in-Publication Data

ISBN 978-0-9829850-6-9

eISBN 978-0-9829850-7-6

TABLE OF CONTENTS

FOREWORD

Tips on how to be smarter, thinner or richer surround us every day. Natalie has gone beyond just telling you what to do. She's showing you how it all comes to reality. In narrating Katherine Murray's journey, she illustrates the true power of the human mind in creating the life of her dreams. Facing her debt and unhappiness, she tackles the root of her problems by looking inward and understanding herself and how she got there. She uses her newfound realizations to grow and transforms her situation to one of comfort, contentment and progress.

You've heard many times of the concept of how your thinking can influence your life. You understand the value of your thoughts. But, you don't understand exactly how it all works. Through Katherine, Natalie shows you how to create productive self-dialogue that can turn the destructive chatter in your mind into useful and fruitful stream of thoughts.

You know about starting with the end in mind and working backwards. Yet, understanding exactly how to bridge the gap between where you want to be and where you are has never been spelled out. This story will show you what this looks like.

These are just some of the tools showcased in the story. This book is packed with many more. All valuable. All can be easily included into your own life. It is a wonderful example of how following a system that others have succeeded from will lead you to your own success, as well.

Enjoy the story, enjoy learning and most of all, enjoy living!
— Loral Langemeier, Five-time Bestselling Author,
Speaker and Coach

DEDICATION

I dedicate this book to my parents, Horst and Joan, for giving me a great chance and sound foundation to build my incredible life from. I also dedicate this book to my husband Glen. Thank you, honey, for being the best husband, partner and life adventurer I could ever have hoped for. Words cannot describe how much I love you.

A MESSAGE FOR YOU

I can remember a time just a few short years ago (early 2006, to be exact) when I stared frustratingly at a table strewn with credit card statements and invoices, wondering what vital piece of information I was missing.

I truly thought I was doing everything right. My husband, Glen, and I were serial entrepreneurs and had owned and operated a myriad of different businesses ranging from a Nightclub to Property Development to Bathroom Advertising to Coffee Franchises. We tried just about everything.

Not only were we business owners and massive action takers, we read all the books, we attended all the seminars, heck, we even walked the burning hot coals at a Tony Robbins event but still the life we dreamed about eluded us. Our reality was hard work, steep learning curves and financial regression, far from the extensive world travel, eating out at fancy restaurants and fancy cars or flashy watches we deemed our benchmarks for success.

Then, in late 2006, I came across a little movie called The Secret, and the penny finally dropped…hard. This was the first time I consciously became aware of The Law of Attraction's existence, and I won't lie, it was a revelation. Learning the dynamics of this universal law and rigorously testing the validity of the information I unearthed soon became an obsession.

I am a logical thinker. I needed scientific proof and undeniable social proof that this law could work and would work for anyone…especially me.

I was not disappointed. Once I realized the truth, there was only one thing to do.

SHOUT IT FROM THE ROOFTOPS!

My obsession quickly bloomed into passion. My life's mission became 'Reach as many people as possible with this message. Help them realize they have complete control over their lives. Life can be as incredible as they dare to design...a life beyond their wildest dreams.'

This is my burning motivation behind writing this book. I want to take you through a story that illustrates how these principles apply to real life. I want to show you what is possible for you once you apply the lessons weaved throughout these pages.

I want to empower you to create a life that's unrecognizable, fulfilling and exceptional that creates a tsunami of positivity influencing those you love and beyond.

Katherine's adventure in this book paints a compelling picture of how using the principles of Law of Attraction and other success skills can empower you to achieve any goal you set yourself. After months of carefully caressing and cajoling this character and her journey I finally removed my fingers from the keyboard feeling confident that the important message that can free the world and propel us all into a new, exciting and outstanding life had been accomplished.

But...it wasn't enough. I had to take things a step further.

Being a logical girl I wanted to explain to you how to use this information to your advantage, down to basics... step one, step two, step three. For me to feel like the Law of Attraction had been conveyed to the best of my ability, it had to be explained as plain English, easy to follow and utterly life changing.

Systemized.

So, while watching Newsroom on HBO one night and hearing the words 'Stay tuned after the show for a look inside the episode with Aaron Sorkin,' an ingenious idea was born.

You will notice at the end of each chapter a heading 'Inside The Chapter.' So, in the same vein as 'Inside the Episode,' 'Inside The Chapter' takes you behind the scenes through the portal of a 'funny looking barcode,' or QR code, and website URL.

When you choose to enhance the chapter you just read by either using a QR Reader app, like Nanoreader, on your mobile phone, which you can download from here: http://www.niywd. com/qr or by typing the website address into your Internet browser, you will meet me.

Well, a video of me, to be precise, taking you inside the head of Katherine, explaining the life lesson she is going through. I explain how this relates to my own personal experience and how you can easily implement this knowledge into your life.

Each video fills in the gaps and constructs a beautiful blueprint that you can use over and over again to achieve ANYTHING you put your mind to. ANYTHING.

These are life skills, success habits, proven principles and well-known strategies of the mega successful. Oprah, Richard Branson, Gabby Douglas and Michael Phelps, just to name a few, all use the information detailed here in the story and extra video lessons. This information is common knowledge and extremely effective for those that use it.

It can be extremely effective for you, too.

My recommendation for 'milking this book for all it's worth' is to read each chapter then go straight to the video that expands the message for you with practical, easy-to-apply (and understand) information that will change your world, once you start living it.

Guaranteed.

You know, since being exposed to the Law of Attraction in 2006, life has changed considerably.

I wake up next to my perfect partner every day. We live in an endless summer shared mostly between Sydney, Australia, and San Diego, California. All of my 'success' benchmarks have been realized. I am making a difference through my life mission and philanthropic efforts. I am living my passion and connecting with some of the most amazing individuals on Earth through my online show, TheInspirationShow.com. I travel the world, eat out when I want, shop for clothes without looking at the price tag and can afford to be generous with family and friends.

The dream life I yearned for has become a life I wouldn't have dreamed up in a million years. To say it far exceeds my expectations is an understatement.

This is what I want for you. You can have it.

The only thing standing between you and the life you want is a bit of knowledge, a pinch of effort, adopting some habits, changing some thought patterns, taking some action and an ounce of discipline.

Are you ready to step into the life you've always dreamed of?

Join me here, and I promise when you apply what you learn here, you can 'Have a life beyond your wildest dreams.'

—Natalie Ledwell

CHAPTER ONE

Coming Attractions

Just breathe, Katherine Murray told herself as she walked with anticipation across the quiet studio lot. *Just breathe and appreciate each moment.* The sun was radiant on this early morning, infusing the still air with warmth and strength. The person sauntering ahead of her disappeared into one of the buildings, leaving Katherine alone as she turned onto a narrow street.

When she reached Studio 9, she triple-checked the studio number against her call sheet. As she pushed open the heavy, metal door of the studio, she breathed deeply. She immediately started to feel the energy, a sharp contrast to the quiet harmony that she had enjoyed moments before. Production assistants, directors, script supervisors, set designers, the lighting crew, and make-up artists scurried around the studio. Someone walking past announced that there was fresh coffee, but the message was drowned out by the buzz of activity. Katherine could just make out the voice of a comedian on the other side of the curtains and an audience chasing his jokes with hearty laughs.

Katherine watched the bustle as she pulled on the beige sweater with pearl buttons that she had brought to complement her tailored slacks and magenta blouse. She

1

stood in the same place, smiling and taking in the action, until a small girl holding a clipboard and coffee came up to her and asked, "Katherine Murray?"

"Yes, that's me." Katherine held out her hand.

The girl whisked the clipboard under her arm immediately and took Katherine's hand. "I'm Megan, first director. It's such an honor to meet you. We are very excited about having you on the show. Shall I show you to your dressing room?"

"Thank you." Katherine followed the young lady around the studio and into a less hectic hallway. A piece of paper with a name written across it was attached to each door, including Katherine's. She took a moment to value this milestone. *My name on the guest dressing room at Diane Craven's studio, she thought. Yep, this is a moment.*

Megan opened the door and showed her inside. The room was simple but elegant. A glass coffee table stood in the middle with a stunning arrangement of flowers demonstrating every color one could imagine. A soft-looking, neutral-colored sofa sat along one wall. Directly across, a mirror hung above a tall chair and counter.

"Katrina is the make-up artist, and she'll be here shortly, along with the producer and director. They'll be going over the talking points for you and Diane," Megan said. She pointed to the small microfridge that stood in a corner. "There's water in there, and if you'd like coffee, food, or anything else, just pick up that phone hanging on the wall and someone will help you."

"Thank you so much, Megan." Katherine beamed at the girl. Megan smiled and headed toward the door. Just before she stepped out of the room, she said, "Oh, and one more thing. I'm following your program myself, and it really does work." She closed the door behind her. Katherine smiled and turned back to take in the room.

One of the walls displayed framed pictures of some of the guests who had appeared on the show over the past thirty years or so. Katherine recognized just about every celebrity and political figure in the photos. Diane Craven was dressed spectacularly in each shot. Katherine always admired Diane, and Diane's show was among the very few that she would actually commit to watching on a regular basis. She admired the quality of discussions and the caliber of the guests. Being here makes sense, Katherine thought. Gratitude filled her as she took another deep breath and sat down in the tall make-up chair.

After talking points were discussed and the final touches of hair and make-up were applied to Katherine's glowing face, she glimpsed her reflection in the mirror and marveled at the subtle touches the make-up artist added to enhance her bright blue eyes and blonde hair. The preparation time was in distinct alignment with what she had envisioned this experience to be. It would make the interview that much more powerful.

Another assistant directed Katherine back stage, and she could feel the vibration of energy that permeated the studio both in front of the curtains and behind. The curtains were set off to the side and were simple black panels that merely served the purpose of separating the live stage from the backstage bedlam. If they were pressed on time, no one seemed fazed. The show was going on just as planned.

Katherine nodded and quietly thanked her escorts. She peeked out a side door to see the audience. Every seat was taken, and the room undulated with enthusiasm. Diane was already on set. She was a handsome woman with striking features. Her hair was perfectly styled. Her clothes, as expected, were incredible. In one hand she held note cards far out in front of her face. In the other hand, she held a wand with a magnifying lens attached to the end. Katherine watched Diane read and smiled blissfully, soaking it all in.

Though Katherine was brimming with energy that had been building since she entered the studio, and although she had jitters of excitement, she was able to maintain a calm appearance. She watched one of the crew members approach Diane and whisper into her ear. Diane turned and looked directly at Katherine. Diane then excused herself from the make-up artist and stood up and walked over, her arms spread wide. "Katherine, it's a true honor. I can't tell you how delighted we are to have you as our guest. How do you feel?"

They embraced awkwardly, both trying to avoid smudging make-up onto the clothing of the other. "I feel fabulous, Diane, thank you. Everyone's been amazing."

"I'm happy to hear that. I'm so sorry I didn't see you earlier. I usually stop by the dressing room and visit before this point, but things don't always go as planned."

Katherine nodded. She knew all too well that things didn't always follow a plan, but she also appreciated the value in that. Very rarely did the positive experiences in her life happen the way she thought they would.

After more welcoming and a brief description of how the show would ensue, Diane pardoned herself to finish with the last-minute touches on her wardrobe and make-up. Katherine thought Diane looked beautiful and felt sincerely privileged and thrilled to be doing a show with this world-renowned personality who had earned respect for her wisdom and compassion across the globe.

Megan came on set again and showed Katherine where she would enter the stage and which chair she should sit in once Diane announced her name. Aware that the cameras would start rolling in a matter of minutes, Katherine felt butterflies of excitement fluttering in her stomach. At the same time, she still felt at peace. It was an odd combination and yet so right for the moment.

Katherine heard the voice of a man from the set direct the cameras to begin rolling. She could see Diane on the television monitor just next to her, standing in front of the audience. A show she'd begun digitally recording on a daily basis was now happening live just steps away—and she was a guest on the show.

"And we're starting in five, four, three, two—"

With a soothing, yet firm voice, Diane began. "You've heard plenty about her. You've watched the movie, and you've even tried it yourself. But the world was blown away when it realized the truth behind this originally fictional story. This tale has literally transformed the lives of people around the world. The woman who wrote the box office hit and world-changing movie *Write Here, Write Now* is in the studio today. Please welcome Katherine Murray!"

The audience stood and clapped, hollered and yelled. There was no doubt they had been waiting for this moment. Katherine couldn't help but smile wide as she walked onto the stage. As if in slow motion, she watched the smiling faces and screaming mouths. It was as fabulous as she had imagined it would be. She greeted Diane with a hug. As she took her seat and waved to the crowd, they began to settle down, apparently eager to hear what she had to share with them. "Thank you so much," she said to the audience and then again to Diane.

"Welcome," Diane said with unconscious professionalism. "We are so happy to have you here."

"I'm delighted to be here," Katherine returned. She was starting to feel more comfortable and at ease.

"Katherine, this is your first appearance since the release of the film," Diane reminded everyone who was watching.

"Yes."

"Now, not only did you write the screenplay for a spectacular film that has caused a swell of positive pandemonium around the world, but there's another reason you, as a screenwriter, have received so much acclaim."

Katherine nodded humbly. "Yes."

"You wrote this movie in one week!"

The audience, being reminded of this amazing feat, shook their heads in amazement.

"Yeah." Katherine remembered back to the moments when she wrote this film.

"I think everyone wants to know, including me... how did you do it?"

Getting a little more relaxed in her chair, Katherine began, "You know... when you know where you're going with anything in your life, you get there much faster. It's like the pedal is to the metal and you just move forward, and there's not much that you let get in the way. If something does get in the way, you take care of it and move on. When I wrote the screenplay, it was so important to me to get the message across that I didn't want to waste any time. As soon as the inspiration came, I was at my computer typing away, and the words flowed."

The audience clapped at Katherine's response.

"You talk about flow, which is a term I often hear writers use. Finding flow is like a magical thing that happens. But, this is a little different. I mean, you wrote this in one week! There's got to be something very special about you. What is it?" Diane smiled broadly at Katherine.

"Well, I think we are all special, and it's amazing what any of us are capable of accomplishing when we believe we can. I just happened to feel so strongly about the message of this movie, and it was as if I couldn't hold it in any longer."

"We're going to talk in more detail later about the moments that inspired you to write this film and about how you managed to have it produced in record time. But before we do, tell us a little about where you came from."

"Well, I have seven siblings and we grew up in a small country town. My childhood was pretty normal. We had two parents who loved and supported us, and I grew up doing what kids did back in those days. I rode bikes, played safely in the streets, participated in sports, and always had someone to hang out with. For those times when I wanted to be by myself, I would write short stories either about what I was feeling at the time or about the fun, luxurious life I would experience in the future.

"I wouldn't say that we were poor, but as you can imagine, money was tight. Everything was very standard and customary in my life. A few of my friends had aspirations of heading to the 'big city' to go to college. However, most people I knew were excited about just getting a job, meeting a partner, maybe traveling a bit, getting married, having kids. You know the drill. But there was something inside me that wanted more, something different, yet I held back. I was attracted to challenges, and I loved being different. I had so much empathy for others, and I was always the one who stood up for the kids who were being picked on.

"My first career in fitness helped me recognize that I loved helping people. It wasn't long before I moved to the big city and broadened my horizons. Things usually worked out for me, so I had the mindset that things would fall into place for me even if I didn't know exactly what I was doing. Those thoughts eventually led me to having what felt like a planned life, which felt very average. I seemed to be resigned to the fact that something different and extraordinary was not in the cards for me. My choices seemed to be based on whatever presented itself or was right in front of me at the time. There wasn't any planning or deliberateness per se. I was just floating along with what life threw at me. Next thing I knew, I was fortyish and divorced with a mortgage and a restaurant business that was sucking the life out of me."

"Well at least you had your own business. That's not so average." Diane laughed.

"The problem is that I struggled with it. I forked out a ton of money to buy a business where I worked longer, harder, and was paid less than any job I'd ever had," Katherine mused.

"I remember being so frustrated and wondering what secret to life I wasn't getting. What I was missing. You know? All my friends were happy and successful, and I couldn't help but wonder if they were keeping some vital information from me. As it turns out, they were."

"Well that's definitely not your situation now," Katherine interjected. "You seemed to have discovered that secret. So many people are in the position you have just described, and they want to experience the success and joy you have created. Wouldn't you say that's key, that you created it?"

"Oh, absolutely. And that's what the movie is about."

"So, you're now an award-winning screenwriter and filmmaker," Diane continued.

"Yes."

"And you've only written one screenplay and made one film?"

"Right," Katherine laughed.

"You have had virtually no experience in this industry, yet you wrote the screenplay in one week and had it made in less than six months. Now, one year later, here you are."

Katherine dipped her head humbly.

"Okay, so tell us why you didn't do any other interviews?" Diane questioned, knowing the audience was hungry for the response.

"You know, I always imagined that one day I would be here on this stage with you." Katherine smiled at the audience. "It was what felt right to me. I felt like the movie was having the effect I really aimed for, and I didn't feel that I needed to do a big PR stint until the timing was right. It was having such a powerful influence that I didn't need to chime in. I knew something astounding would come from it, but even my greatest hopes have been exceeded with the awards I've received and the response from people all around the world. Expressing the message, not my ego, is imperative, and I think that shows in the film. I felt that this time would come, and I knew that being here at this time would be the best choice for me." Katherine took a sip of water.

"And we are so glad you did," Diane said. She looked to the camera. "We're going to take a quick break, and when we return, we'll talk more about how this whole escapade began and what Katherine encountered along the way. You don't want to miss this." Diane waited until the camera lights dimmed and the director confirmed the break.

Go Inside the Chapter:

— Do you sometimes feel drained by negative people or circumstances in your life?

— Do you want to make positive changes in your love life or with your health, career or finances, but you're not sure how to get started?

Scan the code below or go to **www.niywd.com/chp1** to access a free bonus video with author Natalie Ledwell.

Inside, Natalie shares with you the secret Katherine uses in Chapter 1 to welcome more positively charged people and golden opportunities into her life, and how you can too.

Plus you'll get instant access to a free "Happy Blast" gift that you can use to instantly shift yourself into a more happy, positive state of mind anytime you choose, no matter what's going on around you.

CHAPTER TWO

Find Your Happy Place,
It Is the Foundation

When she was young, Katherine dreamed about leading an extraordinary life. She imagined being wealthy, traveling the world, and having exciting escapades. However as she matured, the responsibilities of adulthood came into play. Stress and responsibility dominated her life. She assumed that it was typical for the dreams of youth to fade away, unattained. The once audacious dreams seemed just that, too grand to become reality.

If someone were to ask her to create a wish list, it would be filled with extravagant life experiences and grandiose successes. A wish list, however, seemed to be something that could only come true in a fairy tale. She didn't expect any of her wishes to ever become true.

She was frustrated. Life had taken such a hold on her that she had completely forgotten that she used to dream. Everything was a struggle now; her marriage had failed, she was living month-to-month trying to make ends meet, and the stress of running a business was taking its toll. Sometimes she felt that there was nothing in her life that she could be happy about. How had being an adult become so challenging? Why did everything she touched work out badly? Why couldn't she get it together? Would life ever get easier? How could she get through one more day, let alone a lifetime? Why was she so inadequate? Where were these daunting thoughts coming from? Was she giving them permission to parade through her mind?

There were a load of reasons that impeded her from fulfilling her dreams. She felt incapable. She felt defeated. Life had become sheer survival from one second to the next. It was a bad ride. Where on earth was the exit?

She recalled many of the self-defeating statements that she once told herself: "I'm a failure as a business woman." "My family must be so disappointed in me." "I can only imagine what my brothers and sisters are thinking." "Everything makes me feel irritable." "I am annoyed." "I am unhappy." "I hate my life." She confirmed that she was too old at forty to do anything spectacular and any potential greatness she might have been capable of had long since disappeared. She didn't know enough about technology, which seemed to be where everyone was creating wealth these days. She knew nothing about how to get ahead and solve her financial mess. And when she did discover something that could help her, it seemed that the effort required to put it in motion was too daunting. Was this how life was supposed to be?

Suzette, one of the waitresses who worked for Katherine at her restaurant, suggested she start a gratitude journal to help her out of her funk. *At this point I'll try anything*, Katherine mused.

It was a cold night when she sat on the couch in her living room contemplating her situation, so she wrapped a soft chenille blanket around her legs. She eyed the journal doubtfully as she sipped a cup of chamomile tea. Finally, she set the teacup on the coffee table and opened the journal. The blank page stared back at her. She looked at the teacup then back to the journal. She moved the cup to better suit her reach and focused again on the journal. Nothing! She could write nothing. "Really? Nothing?" she shouted at the journal. She felt pathetic.

The climb out of the mess she found herself in seemed as if it would be a never-ending uphill crusade, so as unhappy as she was, she'd assumed it would be easiest to settle for her current situation.

Her relationships also suffered. She repeatedly initiated ridiculous, false competitions with her siblings and close friends. She always compared her accomplishments to those of others, judging their choices. She always assumed that they were judging her every endeavor, and this perception fueled her desire to fight back and win. She felt so foolish now.

How could she expect to be loved by others so strongly when she was incapable of expressing that same love? If she couldn't show her own family and friends that she loved them, how could she ever do that with a man? When she really thought about it, she realized she was operating in a completely overwhelming state of unhappiness. But that was just the beginning.

The following evening, she jumped into bed with her notebook. She was so angry at her inability to write anything the night before that she was absolutely determined to write something this time. She decided not to be too hard on herself and to simply make a list of everything she was grateful for that day. She was determined to come up with something, even if she listed things she might not usually feel grateful for, such as her ability to write, the blanket on her bed, and the fact that she even had a bed.

It was surprisingly hard, and her heart began to race as she began her first entry. "I am grateful for the socks that are keeping my feet warm. I am grateful that I have a roof over my head." She smiled. It was a short list, but writing it made her feel good.

The next night, she sat down to write again. This attempt yielded two more sentences: "I am grateful to be writing this journal and to have written something at all. I am grateful that I can smile." It didn't take long before she was anticipating these moments at home with her pen in hand rather than fearing what she would write. In no time, paragraphs started to flow from her fingers. "I am grateful that I have nice neighbors. I am grateful that I get to walk through the park on my way to work. I am grateful that my family is healthy. I am grateful that I found a supply store that is cheaper than the one I've been using. I am grateful for..." The list went on and on. As she wrote, she felt a positive energy rising within and realized she was feeling less negative. The more she wrote, the better she felt and the happier she became. This made her want to write. And she did, and that's when things started to happen.

⤳

Music played as the cameras scanned the applauding audience. As it eased down, the cameras revisited Diane and Katherine. "We're back with Katherine Murray, award-winning screenwriter and filmmaker of Write Here, Write Now." She turned to Katherine. "Now, most people are anxious to hear the story about what inspired you to write such a film. An even more intriguing point is how you began this whole journey. Let me first ask you, was creating films something you always wanted to do?"

"When I was a child I loved to write. I didn't particularly think about writing movie scripts, but writing was an enjoyable escape for me. I just thought that writing was a 'cool' activity. Frankly, I thought that if I could earn a living at something that I enjoyed doing like writing, traveling the world, or helping people, then my life would be perfect. Those goals could have manifested themselves in other forms—writing books, writing an influential blog, writing for a travel magazine. Instead it manifested into the creation of this movie.

Diane nodded that she understood Katherine. "Even though I loved writing and had this fascination with it, I never allowed myself to dream that I could become a writer. I was shot down by my own fear. Who actually gets to live the life of their dreams, especially an average person like me?" Katherine giggled. "I mean, I never took any kind of course for writing. The most I ever wrote at the time was a grocery list." The audience laughed. "I mean honestly! I just had no clue, and I wasn't taking any steps to actually learn. I figured I had too many other life responsibilities to worry about. I mean, isn't that what we're supposed to do?" she mocked.

Diane looked to the audience. "I think many of us struggle with similar types of challenges, right? It's not uncommon for someone to claim that they have a passion for something or that they want their life to be a certain way. However, in the end, they fail to make it happen because of fear and worry."

"That's exactly right, and that's precisely where I was and essentially where I needed to be in order for all of this to happen," Katherine added.

"Interesting. You say it's where you needed to be?" Diane asked.

"Oh, definitely. Had I not been so frustrated with the situation of my life and at myself for not doing anything about it, I would have remained in the same place. I thought it was actually easier to try to make the best of my circumstances than to try to change them. I finally realized that if I really wanted a happy, fulfilling life, one in which I could make a difference doing something that I love, then something would have to happen. When I came to accept the fact that it was essential that I make changes, that was the starting point."

Diane announced another commercial break. Katherine looked into the audience again and as the lights shifted, so did her thoughts.

∾

It was late one night several years back. She was sitting alone in her dining room at the round pine table that was, as usual, covered with unpaid bills. At least twice a month she found herself at this table inundated with panic. Her stomach would knot, and her head would pound in defiance. Getting control over her finances seemed impossible, and despair overcame her until she gave in to the exhaustion it caused.

The phone rang, piercing the quiet of that particularly hopeless night.

"Kath? It's Leanne. It's that time of year! Holiday time!" Katherine could hear the excitement in her voice. She wished she hadn't answered.

"Oh, right."

"You missed the last two years. You have got to come this year. We're going to Costa Rica. It's going to be off the charts amazing. Apparently, Allana has the best hookup at all of the nightclubs and restaurants. We won't need to wait in lines anywhere. Can you imagine a full day of doing nothing but lounging in the sun?! I can't wait. Are you in? Please say yes." Leanne seemed to erupt with energy. It nearly wiped Katherine out.

"You know—"

"Katherine! Come on." Leanne pleaded.

"It's just that the restaurant has been really busy, and I can't really walk away from it right now."

"Katherine! They will survive without you."

The real issue was that she couldn't afford to go. Knowing she couldn't join her friends already made her feel left out, embarrassed, and slightly sick to her stomach. She couldn't even remember when she had last had a vacation.

After ending the painful conversation, she imagined Leanne breaking the news to Allana and Jenny, and she felt pathetic. It was enough to make her cry. She thought back to all the years of her pent-up disappointment. All of the times she had missed out on living so she could work—and now here she was with nothing to show for it but more stress and heartbreak. Where did she go wrong? Why was it that all of her friends could consistently afford to do things they wanted to do, like go on vacations, while she couldn't? Wasn't she following the same plan they were? If only the world didn't revolve around money. "It truly is the root of all evil," she said out loud.

The more she thought about how disappointed she was with her financial situation, the more other issues began to surface. Like love. Just the thought of the word made tears stream down her face. Why didn't anyone ever ask her out on a date? It was so easy to blame the breakup of her marriage on her ex-husband. He was the one who cheated. Maybe she had driven him to it. It had been so long since she'd even been on a date that she wondered if there was something about her that people found off-putting.

She desperately yearned to find a person who would be supportive of her and love her. Why did it seem totally impossible? She wondered if the weight she had gained was a turnoff to men. She thought it ironic that she owned a healthy, organic restaurant but survived on fast food. That coupled with her lack of time and motivation, it was no wonder she had put on some pounds.

She gazed at her reflection in the window next to her. It was almost unbearable. She searched the image, looking for life. All that she could find were her swollen eyes, frumpy stature, and ill-fitting clothes. She cried harder. Would she ever feel happy and excited like Leanne? Something big was missing from her life, but she wasn't quite sure what it was. She decided an easy, short-term solution would be to numb these awful feelings.

She walked over to the kitchen cabinet that housed all of her nice drinking glasses, reached towards the back, and pulled out the biggest wine glass. It was her favorite glass at times like this because it held an entire bottle of wine. Somehow, it made her feel better to have just "one" glass of wine on these nights.

She hadn't let herself cry so much in a long time and it was time to stop. She was good at avoiding her situation, and the wine helped, as did zoning out in front of the television. She flipped through the channels while she took bold sips of the wine. After ten minutes, she landed on a PBS special featuring one of those annoyingly happy motivational speakers. *This will do, she* thought. Normally, she would be utterly annoyed by a seemingly phony, impossibly positive person, but she felt so defeated that it seemed fitting to watch. She was already feeling the effects of the wine, which made viewing the special a bit easier.

"Life is a series of choices. Where you are now is a result of the choices that you made in the past." A pretty woman with an Australian accent was standing in front of the camera. The woman seemed so sincere. Her voice was calming, not grating like the others she was accustomed to. Katherine leaned into the television screen as the woman continued.

"Are you happy where you are?" the woman on the screen asked. Katherine thought the woman was looking right into her eyes. "No. No, I'm not," Katherine answered half believing that the woman could hear her.

"Most people don't know it but you are in complete control of the outcomes in your life. Life doesn't have to be a struggle and it doesn't matter where you are now or where you have been. You can create the life you want just by making different choices. If you are not happy right now, all you need to do is set the intention and make the conscious decision that you will be happy from now on no matter what. You can choose differently. It's all up to you and totally within your control."

Katherine listened until the end of the program. After the credits rolled, she turned off the television, her wine unfinished. *So, I just choose to be happy. That's it?* She thought about it more. "I just choose to be happy," she repeated aloud. "So I just choose to be happy!" She was starting to get excited as she said it over and over again. "That's it! I choose to be happy!"

In a flash, Katherine realized that day after day, week after week she was choosing the life she didn't want, the opposite of happiness. She grabbed a piece of paper and a red marker and wrote in large letters, "I choose to be happy." She then walked to the fridge and placed it under a magnet shaped like a piece of corn.

Katherine was feeling very pleased with herself until she looked back at the unpaid bills strewn across the pine table. *How have I forgotten what it's like to be happy*, she wondered. *Why can I never see the metaphorical silver lining*? She tried to recall the last time that she had felt truly happy. Every day felt like a losing battle to something she hadn't consciously chosen to participate in. But she had chosen it. She then caught herself searching her mind for someone to blame for the position she was in. But there was no one.

This wasn't where she wanted to be. This wasn't where she asked to be. Or was it? She focused only on what she disliked about everything. Day after day seemed to be filled with worry. Could she pay her mortgage on time? Could she pay her vendors this month? Was there enough money to cover payroll? How had she managed to lock herself inside this uncomfortable little box of unhappiness?

She thought of the calculator on the dining table that also served as an office away from the tiny, cold, metal desk in back of the restaurant. The numbers on the calculator made her sick to her stomach. How could she make it? How could she continue on like this? She hadn't even paid herself in over a year. She'd been living off of loans and credit cards. She owed money to family members who had rescued her on many occasions. The money she did make was just enough to keep things afloat. At that point, she wasn't sure she could even do that anymore. Her desperate unhappiness was palpable and all consuming. Something had to be done.

⌒∕⌒

"We're back in five, four, three..." Katherine shifted herself back into the velvet chair provided on the contemporary set. Heidi Hegland, another legendary correspondent, was interviewing Katherine this time. Katherine felt particularly stylish in the modish wool suit that had been given to her as a gift by a top designer.

Heidi introduced Katherine to the audience and said, "It was only a couple of years ago that—"

"That I could barely afford my cable bill to watch your show!" Katherine interrupted. The audience laughed, and several people nodded their heads as if they were familiar with the situation.

Heidi also laughed and then said, "Man! You must have been frustrated!"

"Oh, I was. I was struggling, and I had no idea how to get out. I was overwhelmed with financial burdens and even more so with my own array of negative thoughts. I started to feel like my own enemy. My life was looking like everything I *didn't* want it to be instead of everything I did."

"Everything you *did*?" Heidi asked as she cleared the long blonde hair from her face.

"That's right. I wanted to help people and make the world a better place. I wanted wealth, exotic travel, and happiness, yet I was getting the opposite. The problem was, I never focused on what I did want, not that I really knew what that was back then. Everything I wanted seemed unattainable, and all I could seem to focus on was all the reasons I couldn't have what I desired. Instead I talked about how much I disliked where I was in my life. So guess where I stayed?"

The audience applauded, recognizing her point. Heidi nodded and threw one arm in the air as if praising a higher power. She fed the audience like her hot pink skirt fed color to the set.

Katherine laughed at Heidi's energy. "The night that I sat at my dining room table looking at the pile of bills that I couldn't pay was the night that started the change within me. I watched a woman on television whose message made sense to me.

"And what was that message?" Heidi asked.

"I needed to make different choices. I had the power to make my life what I wanted, but as long as I was thinking the wrong thoughts, I would continue to make the wrong choices. In that moment, I realized that I was living what I was thinking. That's when I made my first conscious choice, to be happy no matter what."

Katherine remembered that night, looking around her home after listening to the woman. The house didn't feel like a home. Suddenly, she realized that she could easily turn her situation into an opportunity, like the woman had described.

Her short recollection was broken by loud cries of agreement coming from the audience. "The epiphany I experienced was such a simple answer. I was focused on this dramatic movie looping in my mind about how I couldn't do this and couldn't do that. And it's exactly what was happening every single day. I was, indeed, creating my own reality. I thought my way into that life," she paused. "But I discovered my own power that night, which was the beginning of my new, improved life."

Heidi turned to one of the cameras. "We'll be right back to talk more about this power." The music rose as they cut to another commercial.

Katherine clearly remembered looking into a mirror that night, into her own eyes, and speaking out loud, "I choose to be happy. I come from a good place. I can turn all of this around." She hadn't been completely sure in the moment if she actually believed it, but it didn't matter, because the more she repeated the phrases, the more she started to believe that she had the power to turn her life around.

The show's theme music played again, bringing her back to the moment. The remainder of the interview flowed effortlessly. Even though this was only her second interview, Katherine had been comfortable throughout it. She felt like she had found her groove.

After the show, Katherine's publicist whisked her off to the next venue. She admired the designer outfit waiting for her in the limo. She had one more interview for the day before catching a flight to London. She was a world traveler now. She was in demand, and she was more than happy to share her experience. The timing was perfect.

As a young man powdered Katherine's nose and forehead, she remembered the worries and obsessions that used to fill her head: fear, relationships—or lack thereof, issues with family and friends, poor self-image. It had been a never-ending montage of negativity.

☙

She showed up late one afternoon at the restaurant before it opened for dinner, feeling happier than she had for a while.

She had let a woman pull out in front of her into the heavy traffic, and the woman had smiled and nodded in gratitude. The exchange made Katherine beam.

But then she began anticipating all the negative things that would likely happen that evening. The restaurant probably wouldn't even bring in enough money to cover the night's expenses. All of the problems she would have to deal with and the challenge of making enough money that day consumed her thoughts until she suddenly said to herself, *Stop!* And they did, as quickly as they had started. *I'm really enjoying this happy buzz*, she thought.

She stood in the middle of the restaurant with files in one hand and her purse in the other. As she looked around she thought, *It would make me really happy if the staff would come in on time and in a good mood. I want the chefs to be organized and work as a team instead of yelling at each other. I'd like a full restaurant of happy, smiling customers all leaving generous tips.* She imagined the successful evening unfolding until one of the waitresses interrupted her thought process. "Geez, Katherine! Why do you have such a big smile on your face?"

"Suzette!" Katherine exclaimed. "I was just fantasizing about a problem-free night.

"Wouldn't that be a dream?" Suzette replied as Janelle, another waitress, walked through the door.

"Well, we're off to a great start. You girls are nice and early," Katherine said. Near the end of the evening Katherine realized how quickly the night had breezed by and how she'd even enjoyed a laugh with the kitchen staff halfway through the evening.

"Wow!" Janelle said surprisingly. "This has to be a record night for tips. I'm so glad there was a great crowd tonight."

It was then that Katherine recognized the similarity between her daydream and the way the evening had unfolded. No, she thought. *It can't be. I didn't just create a smooth-running night just by thinking it first. Must have been luck."*

✍

When her makeup was done, Katherine returned her attention to Jason Schulty and the crew. There was no audience on this set. It felt intimate, yet invigorating. The interview seemed to pick up where the other had left off. "What is this power? And do all of us have it?" Jason asked.

"Without a doubt! We all have it." Three cameras zoomed in on Katherine and Jason. "Have you ever noticed that when you watch an uplifting romantic comedy, your mood changes?" Some of the crew behind the cameras nodded. "You might feel more romantic or hopeful when it comes to love. Or how about when you read a book in which the underdog wins and you feel that you can relate to it?" Jason nodded.

"You feel inspired. You have moments after walking out of the theater or putting the book down when you think, 'If they can do it, I can do it!' When you allow positive images and thoughts to consume your mind instead of doubt, fear, and rejection, you move forward." Again, Jason nodded.

"But so often, we let those feelings dwindle, and then the negative images take precedence again. I realized that night at my restaurant that I was creating everything I didn't want because I was so intently focused on how badly I didn't want it. I never let the good, happy feelings stay around. It was no one's fault. I was the one in control. And when I realized that—"

Suddenly, Katherine found herself on another set across the world. She was sitting at a table with three women of different generations and various backgrounds. "Is that when you decided you needed to write?" one of the hosts asked. She turned her attention to the middle-aged lawyer who asked the question.

"Almost. That same day, I ran into an old friend from school. She'd come into the restaurant and acted surprised that I was in the restaurant business. 'I always thought you'd end up writing or something like that,' she said. It was very subtle, but the look of surprise in her eyes struck me. That's when it hit me—"

"What was that?" Lidia, the younger host asked.

"That statement brought back my memory of enjoyment when I was writing. I had completely blocked it out. I pushed away all of the bills and rubbish that lay across my table, and I pulled out my computer and opened a blank document. It was almost as if I needed to prove to her—and myself—that there was something bigger within me. I wrote about how frustrated I was and how miserable I felt. I wrote about my shame and my guilt. It was all bad, but it was a big release of negativity." She paused and made a face that reflected the negative feelings. "And then I did something that changed everything."

"Tell us," Oksana, the oldest of the women, said softly.

Katherine waited a beat as she relived that moment. "I hit the backspace button." The women smiled. Katherine smiled back and said, "And then I changed it. I said, 'why not?' Let's just pretend that what's happening now isn't really happening and that what is going on right now was actually fantastic! If I could influence the events of that night in the restaurant, maybe I could influence other events in my life." The large audience reacted with boisterous applause.

"It was a stretch, and at first I didn't believe myself. In fact, it took a few pages before I could really commit to it. I wanted to see what would happen if I started rewriting the movies that were playing in my mind. I started to create scenes that focused on what I really wanted, and it wasn't long before my mind actually believed it."

Lidia asked, "And do you remember the first scene you wrote?" Katherine did. But more importantly, she remembered what that first scene did for her.

"It was more about how I was feeling. See, I was so frustrated and unhappy, and I didn't want to feel that way anymore. I knew that life wouldn't always follow the plan I laid out. I experienced that firsthand with my business and my marriage, neither of which turned out the way I had hoped. But I didn't know how to handle it when my plans failed. I didn't know how to turn the divergence and challenges into something better, so I kept surrendering to the letdowns. Something started to make sense to me, though. I thought that if I could be happy deep down then I could at least get out of the rut I was in. That's what happy, flourishing people did!"

"And it was something you wrote, like a scene in a movie that made you realize this?" Oksana asked.

"Yes. It was so simple, yet it made me feel so good. I felt like I could take a common situation that I didn't want and turn it around. The first scene I wrote for myself was a simple dialogue between me and my accountant."

"Really?" Puja, the most pensive of the three, asked.

"I knew that I wanted something different, but I didn't know what that looked like. So I started with baby steps. I wrote a scenario that would make a small improvement on my current situation. Once I saw it written out it was easy for me to see it in my mind."

Katherine instantly remembered the scene. She didn't know what the right format was or how it should be written. She just knew how she wanted the dialogue to go and she wrote it in third person as if watching herself, emotionally detached, observing the situation from the outside.

Katherine walks into her office at the back of a small restaurant. Her accountant, MATTHEW, is sitting at the other side of her desk looking at the accounting ledger.

MATTHEW
This doesn't look good. I'm not sure how you'll make rent or payroll this week. You're overdue on all of your bills, and if you don't catch up this month, you'll have a hard time getting your food supplies shipped.

KATHERINE
(determined)
We'll make it.

MATTHEW
You will? Unless you borrow again, I don't see how it will work. You've got too much going out and not enough coming in.

KATHERINE
We'll do it.

MATTHEW
Are you sure?

KATHERINE
We're going to open up early this week for lunch.
We're not limiting ourselves to just dinners anymore.
We're going to call back the leads we have on catering,
and we're going to sell them and book them. We'll get our
deposits and we will pay these bills.

MATTHEW
Okay.

KATHERINE
We're not going to borrow anything anymore either.
We're going to turn this business around and make money
because it's time for me to get a paycheck and for you
to get a raise.

MATTHEW
I'll help with the calls.

KATHERINE
I'll call the staff in early for a meeting and we'll plan
our lunch menu today.

⌒∂

Katherine summarized the simplicity of the scene for women, explaining that even in its uncomplicated state it empowered her to solve a problem. It shifted her way of thinking. When she tried to analyze what was different that day as opposed to any other day, she kept coming up with the same answer— happiness. She felt more confident and had thought of a solution from a completely different perspective. It was a beginning. Instead of the panic and fear scenes that usually played in her mind, she made the scene about solving a problem. As she read it back, the simple dialogue made her feel accomplished and confident.

It was the beginning of seeing herself as a "happy" person, the kind she used to envy. She started to write short stories and play them back in her mind. She created scenes and visions of herself smiling as she got up in the morning, having coffee with her staff, and laughing instead of getting irritated. She thought of her restaurant in a new light with different emotions attached to it. In her mind, she decorated it differently and added authentic flair and meaningful recipes to the menu. She envisioned her customers loving the meals and coming back for more. She saw successful marketing endeavors. She acted as if she were proud of her business rather than ashamed. She continued to write herself and act as if she were a happy, fulfilled person maintaining a successful business. At first she had to pretend, but it wasn't long before happiness was her natural state of mind.

᠊ᢒᢇᠣ᠊

The women were completely intrigued. "In those moments, as simple as the interaction was between me and my accountant, I felt free of fear. I felt like I could solve any issues that might come up. As long as the fear didn't block me, I could see the answers. It was a way for me to emotionally distance myself so I could think more clearly and see a solution much more easily."

Lidia chimed in again, "So, instead of writing about the fear and worry of what you would do and what you felt was happening in your life, you backspaced, erased your current reality, and rewrote it the way you wanted it to go."

"I did, and the more I did it, the more I witnessed myself naturally and painlessly finding a solution to whatever came up until I came to have faith that there was always a resolution."

"Did situations keep improving?" Puja asked.

"You know, Puja, in my perception they did. Creditors started calling me to collect money that I was having a hard time making. I couldn't pay all of the bills, but I was able to make the minimum amounts on most of them. While one problem was getting solved, another would arise. But, it was ok. Once it did, I wrote my way out, and it *would* improve once I took action. I just believed that any challenge I needed to solve would come to me, and I would know how to fix it. Every time I wrote it, I could see it in my mind, and I could feel it as if it were actually happening."

"And did the problems get solved?" Oksana asked.

Katherine smiled. "They did. That's when I noticed that everything I wrote would come to fruition in some way or another. And that, ladies, was a complete thrill. The key was to start from my happy place *then* focus on the solution. That was the power."

"Beautiful," Oksana said to Katherine and then faced the camera. "When we come back, we'll talk more about the film from conception to execution. And later, we will explore why the film is changing lives around the world."

❦

Music played in the studio of Paul Caufield's radio show. Paul, sitting with his headset just over his perfectly groomed hair, leaned forward to Katherine and asked, "Is your story really how it happened? I mean you actually wrote scenes every day, and they would start to happen in reality?"

"Well, the real version didn't play out exactly as I had written it, but the end result was always what I had imagined." Katherine maintained her relaxed position in the chair as sound was being tested.

"What else do you do? There must be something else."

"Our thoughts create our actions. All I'm doing is starting from a 'happy place' and using the best tool for me, writing, to create the thoughts that will bring me to my goals."

"Just by writing?" Paul asked.

"I write them, and I take action on them. I also turn them into short movies, sort of like a coming attraction of what's to come. They're like movies for my mind… mind movies, if you will, and by watching these movies it was easy for me to see, in my mind, the solution play out."

"I have to tell you, in addition to my expertise in radio, I'm a great marketer." Paul had no issues stating his talents. "So I believe in a great gimmick. But after seeing the film and the effect it's had on all of these people... well, it's brilliant! I mean you're here, and I don't let just anyone on this show." Katherine believed it too. Beyond television, Paul's show was the hardest to get on, and she had been invited. The show was so popular on satellite radio that Paul was considered the richest man ever to be on radio. Katherine flew back to New York to make her appearance. Because of the slight inconvenience and inability to record the show at the same time that she was already in New York, Paul and his company treated her to the penthouse of the most expensive hotel in the city and hosted a party in her honor the same night as the show. Her penthouse was filled with swag from all of Paul's affiliates. From expensive watches to certificates for weekend resort stays, Katherine was living large, and it felt as if everything was simply flowing easily to her.

"I want to know more." Paul was almost falling out of the chair with curiosity, and it struck Katherine as funny to see this distinguished man practically sitting in her lap.

"I gather pictures and words and music that are representative of how I want to feel and where I want to be and what I want to happen. I put them together, and I create scripts and lines that reflect the thoughts to make the feelings become reality. Then I watch it. The more I watch it, the more I feel the way I want to feel. The more I feel that way, the better my thoughts are. It's as if I am already where I say I want to be. It allows me to take action but without a lot of effort to actually get there. It's exciting. The movie becomes reality."

Paul gestured toward the wall photos of him with the president, the awards he'd been given, and family vacation pictures. "I'm quite happy with where I'm at, but there's more. Do you know what I mean?"

"I do." And Katherine really did know. As far as she was concerned, she was only tapping a small bit of what she could accomplish, and it was more exciting than ever. This was just the beginning.

"We're coming back!" Someone's voice called into the sound room.

Paul leaned toward the microphone and adjusted his headset. "We'll talk more later?"

Katherine nodded and stayed silent as they were counted in back to the show.

As if nothing had passed, Paul said, "We're talking with screenwriter and film celebrity, Katherine Murray."

Go Inside the Chapter:

— Do you ever feel dissatisfied with a particular area of your life—perhaps your love life, friendships, health or finances—and wonder, "How did I end up here?"

— Do you find that you sometimes blame the people or circumstances around you for your feelings of dissatisfaction or unhappiness?

Scan the code below or go to **www.niywd.com/chp2** to access a free bonus video with author Natalie Ledwell.

Inside, Natalie reveals the destructive inner game that Katherine plays in Chapter 2 – a game that many of us play – that blocks her ability to achieve happiness in her life.

Plus, Natalie shares with you the simple steps you can follow to feel happier and more confident with yourself, no matter who you're with or where you are!

CHAPTER THREE

Ready, Set...
What's Holding You Back?

Emma Thomas came to Katherine's home for the taping of Breakthrough, an evening news program featuring innovators in one-on-one interviews. Emma often joined interviewees in their homes if they were impressive. It was a daylong affair. Katherine was doted on hand and foot by the best make-up artists, stylists, and caterers one could imagine.

The show would air in less than a week, but because it wasn't a live taping, there was some leeway between segments. In order to fix a mishap with lighting, the crew took a longer break. As Katherine walked to the restroom, she looked around at her beautiful home and appreciated the control she now had in her life and the gift of realizing she had it. Up until recently, she would have never in her wildest dreams imagined living the life that she now had.

She remembered how her thoughts used to be like heavy, toxic poison that weighed her down and kept her from dreaming big or dreaming at all for that matter. She was especially thankful that she had reached a point where she realized how tiring those constant negative thoughts were for her and how she had finally had enough.

The realization happened just after her epiphany. She found herself moving forward, but still not reaching the distance she wanted to go. It wasn't long until she found herself falling back into negative thinking and bouts of unhappiness as before. This made her feel worse, because now she knew better. She was staying up late in order to keep the business successful, but she wasn't feeling fulfilled. She knew she wasn't enjoying it. The only time she felt energized and alive was when she was writing. She knew the importance of feeling happy, so she figured that she had two choices: either to stay and be happy or sell and be happy.

The problem was that she couldn't see a way out of her current commitments. She had so many financial responsibilities tied to the restaurant that she felt stuck. Besides, who would buy a restaurant that was barely breaking even? There were so many reasons that she hated being there that she couldn't see the value in the place. It was like she was blinded by her own negative, toxic thinking.

Stay and try to be happy was the choice she took. She decided to at least be grateful that she had her own business that was beginning to thrive. Really, things were picking up and she was surviving better than some people. She took comfort in realizing that it could be worse.

Her thoughts had begun to make real-life changes, and she was definitely happier. Her life was becoming lighter. Even though she had made those changes, she couldn't quite grasp that she had other options, and she also hadn't known how easily her mind would automatically go toward negative chatter. No matter how many times she told herself to make new decisions, she felt like something was inside her holding her back, telling her she couldn't move forward.

It was around this time that Katherine met her friend Jenny for lunch at a local cafe. "You keep saving yourself from the problem in front of you, which is great. But, where do you want to go? What do you really want?" Jenny was known for her forthright attitude. In fact, for most of Katherine's life, Jenny had no qualms about letting Katherine know what she really thought.

"What do you mean?" Katherine set down her water glass.

"You're limiting yourself."

"I am?" Katherine swallowed hard.

"You solve the day-to-day problems at the restaurant, which is great! You've grown the business. You've cut down on expenses, and you'll probably be able to sell it and save yourself from an enormous amount of debt. But then what? What do you want?"

"I don't know. I suppose I haven't gotten that far yet!" Katherine exclaimed.

"Well, how about writing for a living? You do seem to have come alive since you have been writing regularly," Jenny said.

"Yeah, right. I'll become a starving author at the age of forty. I don't think so. If I wanted to do that I should have attempted it in my twenties. That boat has sailed, sister."

"I don't know if you've noticed but there's usually a big 'but' whenever you think about improving your situation. You always have some reason why it's probably too bold a move right now. Do you ever consider more daring goals?"

Katherine wrote every day. But she didn't write about ultimate life goals, the ones that actually made her heart beat faster. She probably didn't write about them because she had no idea what they were. "Well, I guess I haven't gotten to that point yet."

"What do you want? And why aren't you doing it?" She looked deep into Katherine's eyes. "You, my friend, have a limiting belief, maybe more than one." Jenny didn't sugar coat anything, and it was just what Katherine needed in this moment.

"A limiting belief? What do you mean by that?" Katherine was starting to feel a little frustrated.

Jenny lowered her voice and leaned over the table. "Have you ever considered that maybe you don't believe you can have what you want? Could that be the reason you don't write about these things?"

Katherine was quiet for a while. She thought back to her daily writings and habits. She'd come so far, but was she going as far as she could? Was she playing it safe? She wrote every day about a sticky situation that was unpleasant and would actually turn into something better, but that was as far as she went. Maybe on some level she knew that she wanted something bigger, but at this moment that was just a dream.

"I don't know," she said. She didn't have an answer just yet.

"Remember how for years I thought that I couldn't play sports because of my asthma? My mother kept me away from any activity where I might have to exert myself," Jenny stated.

"That's right. But hold on, you run marathons!" Katherine had forgotten how inactive Jenny was when she was younger. She realized she had never heard this story before. She felt guilty for forgetting that the woman who she considered to be in exceptional physical shape had overcome great challenges to get there.

"I do now, but I thought I couldn't. I never did anything. I believed that I wasn't cut out for it and that my body prevented me from doing something I thought I would love." Jenny took a big gulp of her sparkling water. "My weight started to climb and my doctor asked what I did to stay in shape. I had no answer. I did nothing. I thought I couldn't. That was the day he introduced me to breathing aids and a training plan that would increase my lung capacity and prevent attacks. If they should occur, he had me prepared. But I still had a hard time believing that I could engage in any cardiovascular activities."

"What changed?" Katherine asked.

"Once I realized that my beliefs were the problem, I had to clear my mind of the limiting beliefs that kept me from doing it. I started doing research on what I needed to do to start believing that I had no limits."

"And?" Katherine's mind was rapidly taking notes.

Jenny smiled at Katherine's impatience and appreciated her zeal. She reveled in thinking that Katherine finally may have reached the point in her life where she could receive information and take action. "I had to reprogram my brain so that I could form new beliefs that would benefit me and allow me to move forward rather than hold me back. But, before I did that, through my research I began to understand how these limiting beliefs first came to be. It was quite a relief, actually, to realize that everyone has them through no fault of their own. Then through a simple exercise, I was able to reprogram my mind to think differently."

"Can anyone do this?" Katherine entertained her own doubts.

"Absolutely. Anyone can do it. But so many don't because they don't know how."

"Tell me!" Katherine cried.

"First let me explain how limiting beliefs are formed. From the day you were born, actually, from the time that you were growing inside your mother, you were acutely observing and evaluating your environment. Your mind was actually operating in completely different brain-wave states."

"Huh?"

"Just listen. From the womb till the age of two, you are predominantly in delta brain-wave state. This is known as the more primal brain activity that operates from an area of instinct. Because you are limited in conscious thought and communication skills, you are completely operating on instinct at this stage."

"Okay."

"You know what's really cool about this is how much scientists know about our receptivity while we're still in the womb. Did you know that every emotion has its own chemical makeup?"

"Um, no."

"It's true," Jenny said. "Even the chemical makeup of tears of joy and tears of sadness are completely different. The fetus has to prepare itself for the environment that he or she is about to be born into, so he or she processes the emotions of their mother as part of this development. See, it's instinctual!"

"Right." Katherine nodded.

"You understand that as children, we are sponges, right?" Jenny asked.

"Well, I've always heard the expression, but I guess there's more to it than I thought?"

"There is. Between two and six years of age, children are operating in predominantly theta brain-wave state, or 'sponge mode' as I like to call it. In this stage of life, children observe their surroundings to learn how to act and respond.

"A perfect example that we have all witnessed is when a child falls over. The first thing they do is look around to see how the adults are responding to their fall. If mommy's laughing, the child gets up and laughs. If mommy is freaking out, saying things like, 'Oh my God, honey, are you okay? You okay?' the child starts crying.

"We are exceptionally impressionable at this age and we don't miss a thing. As five-year-olds, we form opinions about things like money, health, self-confidence, and love, among other things, that influence us for the rest of our lives.

"You see, this is the time when kids soak up and retain everything they've observed. You didn't sift through it and you didn't make a decision or judgment about it. You just accepted it. You then responded to everything in an automatic way because it was programmed into your subconscious."

"I think I'm starting to understand," Katherine said.

"So in my situation, my mom told me when I was very young that I couldn't exert myself with exercise. I just took that for granted and it became my truth."

"Right. Right." Katherine was completely engrossed.

"When children are told they're tubby, when they observe parents stressing over money, when a child is told they are smart but not very pretty, that also becomes their truth for life and all actions and decisions they make moving forward are influenced by this belief they developed as a child. What I'm saying is that you had beliefs that were already formed between birth and age six."

"Okay," Katherine said.

"So from that point on, everything you experienced strengthened those beliefs that had already formed in your subconscious mind."

"Wait a minute. Are you saying that I am still functioning from the same core beliefs I formed when I was six?" Katherine asked.

Jenny grinned. "You got it."

"So—"

"So, it's time to change those. Just like you choose to be happy, you can choose a new belief system. Most people are adults responding to situations from the beliefs of a six-year-old."

"How did you change the beliefs you had had for so long once you understood that?" Katherine asked Jenny.

"It was pretty simple, really. First, I became aware of and wrote down the negative, limiting thoughts that entered my head, especially when I was working toward a goal." Jenny watched as Katherine nodded, processing the information. "Then I wrote out a new list, the opposite of those thoughts, the thoughts I *wanted* to have when striving for those goals. I made sure they were written as if they were already my normal thoughts, as if I were thinking them right then."

"Then what happened?" Katherine asked.

"That list was very powerful. I read it every day. Through repetition, imagining the 'new me,' and acting like these were my normal thoughts, they eventually became my natural thoughts. From that point on I started to visualize myself running, dancing, jumping, and doing anything that would get my heart racing. I could feel each breath flowing in and out of me with effortless ease. In my visualizations, I could run forever. When doubt came, I would immediately go to these reveries in my mind, and they felt so real. My mind and my body were experiencing the actual feelings of elation and physical freedom." Jenny seemed to have lost herself reliving her life-changing experience.

"It's like me when I write my movies," Katherine added.

"Yes, exactly. And now it's time to figure out how to do that with the bigger dreams, Katherine. Don't limit yourself to just one thing. There's more. There's happiness, there's money, there's adventure, and there's love." Jenny looked deep into Katherine's eyes. "What are you afraid of? Success?"

Katherine sat back in her chair and sipped from a glass of wine. She put the glass down and trailed the mouth of the glass with her fingers as her mind carried her back to her youth.

Once she had it, she brought her attention back to Jenny. "Success was what happened to other people. It was out of my reach. Since it never seemed like an option for me, I rationalized that money and fame were for pretentious people. I didn't need either. I thought that people with money were arrogant and ungrateful. But more than anything, money just seemed too hard to attain. I had no example in my immediate sphere of influence, or knew anyone who had achieved a high level of success, so I didn't even know becoming wealthy was an option." She shrugged her shoulders at the foolishness of it.

"Why did you believe that success and wealth were bad? Can you remember something specific?"

Katherine closed her eyes, remembering when she was five years old. "There was this boy in Kindergarten. His name was Alex, and I remember I really liked him. I remember feeling embarrassed about my clothes. I wore hand-me-downs from my siblings. At recess, Alex made fun of my shoes and the shirt I was wearing, telling me that they looked old and dirty. It made me cry. He told me that I wasn't cool, and I remember he was wearing the latest Nikes and a Billabong shirt, brands we could never afford. When I got home that day, I told my mother, and she told me I should stay away from nasty people like Alex. She said they didn't appreciate things like our family did. She said that having too much made you lose appreciation for what you had. I guess I always believed that if I had success or money, it would mean that I wouldn't appreciate anything."

"Wow." Jenny smiled and nodded. "But, you see the silliness in it now, don't you?"

"I guess I do now. Obviously, when I look back now, I realize that my mom was telling me to stay away from people who would tease me. I interpreted that as "stay away from rich people." I mean I just didn't think about it, and it became ingrained in my thinking. I figured that having wealth must be nice for those people, but I assumed that they were probably genuinely unhappy and didn't appreciate things like I did since I had to work much harder for them. That's what I truly believed." Katherine was almost embarrassed at her own words, but she felt the need to tell Jenny everything now that she understood it.

"Do you think this belief is true?" Jenny asked.

"Now that I've actually become aware of it, no. I don't feel it's true at all."

"Do you understand what's happening in your life because of that limiting belief?" Jenny asked.

Katherine answered quietly, "It's held me back."

"And do you realize what changing that belief could do for you?"

"Most definitely!"

"So unteach yourself this belief."

"Is it that easy?" Katherine asked.

"Absolutely. You already know it's silly. You know that it makes no sense. You know that you're still clinging to a perception you formed as a five-year-old. Do you think every person who has money and success is unhappy?" She lowered her chin and widened her eyes. "Really?"

"No, you're right."

"Every time these thoughts come, stay aware and witness them because, at that moment, you can change them." She paused and then said, "Write it out, Kath. Let it all out on paper." Jenny's voice became softer. "Let yourself feel happy about the abundance you will have, because it will come."

That evening, after a long day, Katherine closed the restaurant late, feeling the same despair she had felt not long ago. Her conversation with Jenny, while alleviating in a way, left her feeling like she had a huge task in front of her. An army of negative thoughts ran through her mind constantly.

"That's a long face you've got there," Ryan, the head chef acknowledged.

Katherine sighed. "Just as I thought things were getting better, I find myself feeling overwhelmed and hopeless again."

"Why so?"

"To tell you the truth, this is just not what I want to be doing, day in and day out. It just doesn't fulfill me." She watched Ryan sharpening his knives. "Oh, please don't take that the wrong way. You're amazing Ryan, and so is everyone else here. I can see that you love cooking and coming in here every day and I couldn't run this place without you. I'm truly grateful, but I just don't feel satisfied."

"So why do you have to keep doing it?" Ryan asked.

Katherine looked deep into his eyes. Her mouth opened to speak, but she kept starting and stopping every time she tried to say something. She had a long list of reasons why she had to do it. But once she opened her mouth to verbalize them, they all seemed like pathetic, lame excuses. Ryan raised his eyebrows at her hesitation.

After Ryan checked out, Katherine was left alone at the restaurant, which was often the case. She pushed in the chair she had been sitting at and walked into her back office. The sign she had pinned to the office wall was the first thing she saw: "I choose to be happy."

"That's right," she murmured to herself. "I choose to be happy. What will make me happy right now?" She began organizing the disheveled office. "It's as cluttered as my life," she observed aloud.

She threw away the trash and filed the papers spread across her desk. "I'm tired of feeling like everything is in disarray. I'm sick of thinking that I'll never amount to anything or that I'm not worthy of success. I'm sick of feeling like a slave to the excuses that keep playing over and over in my head. Surely life isn't supposed to be this hard. From now on, I'm making changes. I'm not thinking that way anymore."

By the time she was done with the rant, her small back office looked like a new room. She hung up the photos that her friends sent to her that made her smile. She put everything into a new designated spot. She could immediately feel the new energy flowing. She vowed that the next day she would bring in flowers to place on her desk.

She was filled with excitement as she moved about her new open space. She felt a warm sense of comfort within herself as she looked around the remodeled office. She hoped the rejuvenated space would help productive thoughts flow more efficiently. Suddenly the negative thoughts felt like heavy rocks to her, and she realized that she needed to exorcise them from her head.

She sat at her clean desk, took out a piece of paper, and began writing down her recurring negative thoughts. Committing them to paper made her feel like she was taking control over them. She could now recognize what had been keeping her down. With each negative thought she listed, she felt as if she were purging and cleansing her mind. It was difficult at first, but after the first few lines, it became easier. It felt like dominos falling; each thought spurred another and that one another and so on.

She then listed the negative thoughts she had when she talked about finding her soul mate. These came effortlessly, and she wrote furiously.

There aren't enough good guys out there.

All the good ones are married already.

I need someone who understands me.

Guys are just after one thing.

I've been hurt before, I'm scared of getting into another relationship.

He'll probably get bored with me after a few weeks.

My parents are right. I will never get married again.

I'm not happy enough to be in a relationship,
who would want me?

I'm overweight and no one would be attracted to me.

I'm not worthy of someone else's love.

She stared at the last sentence on the page. "Oh my god! I don't think I'm worthy to be with a man." She stared into space, realizing what she had been saying all of these years. "No wonder I never get asked on a date! If I don't love myself, how can anyone else love me? I know I wouldn't want to be with someone who didn't love himself."

A wave of sadness, relief, and resolve washed over her. "Oh well, I can only get better from here," she laughed as she leaned back in her chair. Katherine remembered her conversation with Jenny that day and stared up at her "I choose to be happy" banner and then back to her list of negative thoughts.

"I choose to be happy!" She sat up tall. "I'm choosing new thoughts that don't sabotage my success and make me feel miserable."

She drew a line, dividing the page with the list of negative thoughts on the left. At the top of the right column, she wrote in capital letters, "I am worthy of love." As soon as the pen stopped writing, she thought, *Yeah sure you are, you pudgy, lazy*— she cut the thought off. *Wow, I had no idea that my inner chatter was so bad. I really need to remain vigilant.*

The truth of the matter was, at that time, she truly didn't believe she was worthy of someone else's love. *I will be, though*, Katherine promised herself that day. *I just need to keep focusing on the good thoughts, the ones I want to think. It will be just like when I pretended to be happy and then suddenly I was.* She continued to write.

There are plenty of men out there.

My soul mate is waiting for me.

There are many men interested in being with me.

I want love.

She stopped there. Just looking at that list made Katherine feel excited. The short list had untold power in it, just as her other writing did.

This process felt so invigorating that she decided to tackle another area of her life that needed improvement, her health.

I'm too old to be skinny again.

I should be happy with the way I look.

It's too hard to get up early to exercise. Every time I do,
I get injured.

I eat healthy food, but still I can't lose weight.

Maybe it is too late for me to look good.

Size 12 is not fat anyway.

The right guy will love me the way I am.

I'm doing everything right; maybe I don't deserve to be thin.

Again, like a two-by-four between the eyes, it hit her. "Why am I so hard on myself? Where are all these Katherine-bashing thoughts coming from?" she asked out loud.

She found it difficult to remember a time when she didn't think like this. She asked herself, *Seriously, Katherine why do you judge yourself so harshly? You're not worthy? You don't deserve? Where did that come from?*

The first line of the right-hand column was the hardest to write.

I love myself.

"Hmm," she mused. "Obviously this one will require a lot of work." She continued with the list, asking herself what it was that she truly wanted.

I want energy.

I want to be fit.

I want to be healthy.

I want to feel beautiful.

She was beginning to feel more comfortable with this, so she figured she might as well tackle money. This time, the list was easier to start. *I still can't believe I've let beliefs I formed as a five-year-old guide my decisions up until now,* she said to herself.

She remembered how she would ask for money to buy candy. More often than not, her mother would automatically respond, "Money doesn't grow on trees, you know."

Actually she couldn't remember her parents saying *anything* positive about money. Money seemed to be the topic of every stress and argument in the household. Dad was always working to earn more and Mom was always trying to stretch a dollar as far as it could go. She wondered why she hadn't inherited that trait from her mom. "It would have been handy a few hundred times in my life!" She scoffed and shook her head. She wondered if she didn't have any money because her parents had never had money. She had never been given an example of how to create wealth. *Money is just like sand through my fingers. I never keep it for long.* She knew these words were a cop out, an excuse she used to explain her lack of wealth. She stopped herself. *Aha! There are the negative thoughts that Jenny brought out in me. Of course I won't have any money if I hold the belief that I can't make it and keep it!*

"From now on, I believe I deserve wealth. Yeah!" Katherine said out loud and began writing.

I want to have more money than I need.

I want to pay my bills easily.

I want to be able to buy anything I want whenever I want.

After hours of writing, Katherine folded up the paper and stuck it in her purse. She put her pen back in the desk drawer and turned off the lights to the office and restaurant. This time she smiled and said goodnight to the establishment that would somehow bring her satisfaction. She didn't know how, but she trusted in the result.

The director called for the return to the set, and Katherine quickly dried her hands. Remembering the conversation with Jenny and how she had taken action made her grin. She had taken in the scene and her life at that moment, and she felt sincere gratitude that she had trusted in the future—and Jenny.

Go Inside the Chapter:

— Do you find that, despite your best efforts, you just can't seem to create the kind of results you want in your love life, health, career or finances?

— Do you sometimes find yourself preoccupied with negative, critical thoughts about yourself or others?

Scan the code below or go to **www.niywd.com/chp3** to access a free bonus video with author Natalie Ledwell.

Inside, you'll discover how Katherine's negative inner critic (and possibly yours too!) sabotages her happiness and success in Chapter 3.

You'll also learn Natalie's proven, easy step-by-step process that you can follow to silence your negative inner critic and achieve more peace, calm and happiness in your life!

CHAPTER FOUR

Law of Attraction 1, 2, 3

After Emma Tomas's crew had finally finished packing up, Katherine decided to take a walk to clear the cobwebs and decompress after a tiring day. During her walk, she remembered that when she had changed her thoughts, small positive changes had taken effect that had been significant, but still not significant enough. Her incentive had continued, and she had started to find solutions to the problems that were making her business so troublesome.

One evening during an outdoor dinner at her favorite bistro, Katherine had just finished telling Jenny about the woman she saw on the PBS special who had made a life-changing impact on her.

"So, how's that working out for you?" Jenny asked.

"Well, nothing big has really happened or changed yet, but I'm hopeful!" Katherine plastered a big, fake smile across her face. At the very least, she did feel hopeful. "I've been practicing correcting my negative thought patterns and choosing to have positive thoughts instead. Just like you told me to do."

"Oh my God! Finally!" Jenny bursted.

"Huh?" Katherine was confused. "What do you mean?"

Jenny leaned in. "I have been busting to tell you something for years, but I just knew you weren't ready to hear it. Every time I tried, you never actually took my advice. Now you've taken it, and now I can finally tell you!"

"Really? Okay, tell me." Katherine couldn't wait. She was a little dismayed that Jenny thought she wasn't ready to hear whatever it was and that she'd kept a secret from her for so long, but she blew that feeling off and focused on what she was about to learn from her closest friend.

"Have you ever wondered why you have struggled for so long? Have you ever wondered why it is that Leanne, Allana, and I have achieved so much success in our lives?"

Katherine was silent as she gained enough courage to admit that she'd been agonizing over this very question for years, all the while beating herself up over it. "Well, yes," she said with humility.

"Do you want to know why?"

"Um, yes!" Katherine started to feel less embarrassed.

"Okay, the reason we all get pretty much anything that we set our minds to is because we know the secret of a universal law." Jenny smiled.

Katherine felt very left out that all of her best friends had a secret to success that they hadn't bothered to share with her.

"We've been using this knowledge to our advantage for years now," Jenny said.

Katherine's mind swam with thoughts. She wondered if this was what the woman had been talking about on TV. She recalled her friends' achievements and how each had made her feel envious. "You've kept this from me all these years?" Katherine looked down at the table and then back up to Jenny. "You could have saved me all that heartache and struggle. I can't believe it." She wasn't sure whether to be sad, angry, or grateful.

"Kath, you could have saved yourself from all the heartache and struggle. We actually did try to tell you many times, but you never really listened or understood. You heard us talk about visualizing our new businesses. Remember Allana's vision board for her new home? We've always talked about 'putting it out there' and asking the universe for the right event or person to come into our lives. And I know you've heard me talk about something as if it's already happened. Remember when I used to brag about my new car?"

"The Mercedes?" Katherine asked.

"Yeah."

Katherine could vividly remember it now. Jenny used to describe driving in her beautiful Mercedes even before she bought it. "Mmm, can you smell that new leather? It's so fast and powerful. I love driving my dream car." It wasn't long before she had actually been able to buy the car of her dreams.

"What about Leanne?" Jenny went on. "Do you remember how badly she wanted a baby and couldn't get pregnant for almost two years?"

Katherine nodded as she thought of Leanne and her beautiful daughter.

"She used the law to her advantage and look at her now." It was almost as if Katherine was watching a movie.

She could see the montage of all of their successes and how they had come together. She could hear them talking about it, and in her mind, she flashed forward to them finally having it. She could also see herself in those same conversations, complaining about her own circumstances.

She could remember thinking that she must not deserve what they had, and that's why she wasn't getting it.

Jenny watched Katherine and knew what was happening. "We tried to tell you before. We really did. Finally, we knew you just had to be ready to hear it. We knew the time would come. Now you're listening and now I think you're ready."

Suddenly, Katherine felt remorseful for discounting them and labeling their conversations as "Woo woo, crazy hippie talk."

"Can you help me?"

"Don't I always?" Jenny laughed.

Katherine smiled with gratitude, "Even when it's tough to hear, you always do."

"Well, I am going to be tough on you right now." Jenny's face was deadly serious. "Here is my proposal. If I spend time coaching, supporting, and helping you, you have to promise me that you will reach your goals regardless of how hard it seems or how much you think you can't do it. I will help and support you all the way, but you cannot give up. Deal?"

"You'll be with me all the way?" Katherine asked.

"Yes, I will be with you, but you have to enter into this with the mindset that you will do whatever it takes and you will reach your goals. Clear?" Jenny wanted Katherine to completely surrender to the fact that she would have to work for it, knowing that the rewards would be worth it.

"Okay, I'm in," Katherine said with a firm nod.

"Right then! On your feet and raise your right hand," Jenny announced as she stood herself.

"What? No, that's silly. We're in a crowded restaurant. Sit down." Katherine said, half hiding her face so other diners couldn't recognize her.

"Katherine, if you can't perform the first step, then I'm sorry, but I can't help you. You will be facing bigger issues and stepping further outside your comfort zone than simply standing up feeling a bit silly in a restaurant. What's going to happen when you really hit an obstacle? I thought you promised you would do what it takes," Jenny said.

"Is this some kind of test?" Katherine knew Jenny wouldn't sit down no matter how much she begged her to. Jenny seemed to be fearless and clearly didn't care what other people thought. *Maybe that's why she's successful and I'm not. I don't even want to stand up in front of strangers*, Katherine thought to herself.

"Seriously, Katherine. If you can't do this, don't bother wasting your time or mine. Just call it quits before you even begin."

"Alright, alright," Katherine complained as she rose to her feet. "Talk about tough love. I better start getting used to this, I suppose."

"You know that's why you love me," Jenny said and grinned. "Now raise your right hand and repeat after me. I, Katherine Murray…"

"I, Katherine Murray," she said, raising her hand.

"Do hereby state my intention and give my personal promise…"

"Do hereby state my intention and give my personal promise." Katherine could feel the stares of strangers burning holes in her skin.

"To listen and apply the knowledge Jenny teaches me."

"To listen and apply the knowledge Jenny teaches me." Now, there were definitely audible snickers.

"I will do whatever it takes to complete my goals. Failure is not an option." Jenny was enjoying watching Katherine squirm.

"I will do whatever it takes to complete my goals. Failure is not an option."

"I do this for myself and to be an inspiration to the people I love."

"I do this for myself and to be an inspiration to the people I love." Katherine appreciated the weight of the last two lines and sat down as Jenny did. "What, a simple pinky promise wouldn't have sufficed in this situation?" she asked.

"Katherine, a pinky promise would not have served this purpose. First, I needed you to set a serious intention. How many times in the past have you started to lose weight or started to find a guy or started to improve your financial situation and never followed through? You just declared to me, God, and a roomful of strangers that you are not going to quit. Failure is not an option. Those were serious words that carry a serious promise, and when you think of giving up, I'll just replay the audio I sneakily recorded on my phone." Jenny laughed she moved her phone out of Katherine's reach.

"You!" Katherine gasped.

"Oh, and the other thing, you need to get outside of that comfort zone of yours. You've been stuck in there for as long as I can remember. How is *that* working out for you?" Jenny quipped.

"Hah, hah. Very funny. So what is this universal law?"

"It's called the Law of Attraction, or LOA. The basic premise of this law states that if you can conceive the thought of what you want and see it in your mind as if it already exists, and if you feel the emotions of living this, then if you take action in that direction, it will become a part of your reality."

"That doesn't sound too hard," Katherine said.

"Well that's the basic premise. For you to effectively apply this law to your advantage requires some changes to your thought processes. There are certain steps you can take and particular habits you can adopt to ensure that you consistently use this law to positively influence your life. Fortunately, these steps and habits can be accomplished easily by anyone, but it takes effort and discipline in the beginning. It also takes time. But the more you change your thoughts and make some modifications to your everyday routine, the more you realize that you can have anything. You're off to a good start by maintaining a state of happiness and identifying the thoughts you want to have. Now you just need to figure out what you really want, not just what you want to avoid." Jenny raised her eyebrows, satisfied with her point.

"I get it, and you're right," Katherine admitted. "I am," Jenny said.

"You are. I've been focusing on getting my life to a point where the stress would be gone and I could feel like I have a life again."

"Which is great!" Jenny encouraged.

"It is. But, you're right, I want to move forward." "What do you want?" Jenny asked.

"I have been thinking about this question since our last conversation, and I've even been writing down my wants. I want to help people. I want to create. I want to write. And while I'm at it, I want love. I want someone to share my experiences with! I want to be skinny and fit again, I want money, and I want to travel. I want to meet interesting people from around the world, and I want to… I want to go skydiving!"

Jenny laughed as she watched Katherine's exuberant tangent. "Okay let me phrase it this way. If you had a million dollars and knew you couldn't fail, what would you want? Because by using the techniques that I'm going to give you, you can have it." Jenny waited for Katherine to fill in the quiet pause, watching her as her mind was swimming with possibilities.

"Okay, then. What do I do?" Katherine asked her dear friend.

"Well, one of the essential ingredients of using the Law of Attraction to your advantage is the ability to see yourself in your mind's eye already possessing the things you want.

This is called visualization. For someone like yourself, who is not practiced at visualization, it helps immensely if you can organize your thoughts about the things you want by writing them out as present tense affirmations."

"Affirmations?" Katherine queried.

"Yes, affirmations. They're short statements about the goal you want to achieve written as if they have already happened. When your thoughts are organized like this you simply read your list, close your eyes, and visualize what it's like to already have these things." Katherine nodded as Jenny spoke.

"The language we use when writing these affirmations is very important because the wrong language could have us creating exactly what we *don't* want!"

"Okay, let's press pause on this conversation for a second while I grab a pen and paper. I've wasted enough time already, and I definitely don't want to attract more bad stuff," Katherine exclaimed.

Jenny watched as Katherine eagerly fumbled through her purse, asking the waitress if she could borrow a pen and something to write on. "Easy tiger! I won't forget this information in the next few minutes," Jenny laughed.

"Right. I'm ready. Hit me with everything you've got." Katherine was so excited to be learning what she needed to take herself to the next level in life.

"When you break it down, there are actually five types of affirmations you should list that will make visualizing the life you want incredibly easy. The first is describing the things that you want."

"Like, I want to write," Katherine asked, excitedly.

"Not exactly. When you state that you *want* to write, it keeps you in that space of always *wanting* to write. The best way to write this affirmation would be, 'I am a successful writer.' Can you see the difference?" Jenny asked.

"Yes, I can. So basically, I'm stating that I am a writer even though I'm not yet, right?"

"That's right. When you write it as if it has already happened and especially when you start the affirmation with the words 'I am,' it makes it easier for you to picture yourself as a successful writer."

Katherine realized that she'd been writing what she wanted to have instead of writing it like it had already happened. "Got it. So this was an example of the wrong language to use?" Katherine asked.

"Precisely! You also want to make sure you eliminate the words 'no,' 'don't,' and 'not' from this list. When you write your affirmations for your financial goals, writing 'I have no debt' will only have you attracting more of it. What do you think of when you say the word 'debt'?" Jenny challenged.

"Umm, I see the bills piled up on my desk."

"Right. Now what do you see when you say 'abundant' or 'abundantly rich'?"

Katherine imagined seeing a million dollar balance in her bank account, a beautiful home, a sleek sports car, trendy clothes, stunning purses, and a drawer full of expensive watches.

"I understand. So, only write down the things I want and don't articulate what I don't want. I wouldn't write, 'I'm stress-free' because that statement has the word stress in it. Instead I would write, 'I feel happy and content.'"

"You're getting the hang of this very quickly," Jenny commended. "Think of the scenes you wrote. You wrote those as if they were actually happening—"

"Oh, I really get it now!" Katherine beamed, and Jenny laughed at her excitement.

"Now the second type of affirmation on your list is one that describes what life is like now that you have reached your goals, in your case, what it's like to be a successful writer."

"Well, I don't have a clue what that life would be like," moaned Katherine.

"That's why this exercise is critical if you want to create this life for yourself. You don't need to see the whole picture just yet. Start with the easy stuff, like if you were a successful writer, what would a day in your life look like? Would you be able to sleep in? Where would you write? How much time per day would you spend writing? What would you do when you weren't writing? Having lunches and dinners? Who would you hang out with? Would your circle of influence include other writers?"

"I would definitely be sleeping in and having a leisurely breakfast out each morning. I imagine I would write for maybe six hours a day, and ideally I'd like to write in a place where the scenery from my window is inspiring and natural sunlight fills the room. I would love to hang out with other writers so we could exchange ideas and so I would have support from people who knew what I was going through." Katherine was drifting off into a wonderful scene.

"Great," chimed Jenny. "So, how would you write this into affirmations?"

"Let's see, maybe something like, 'I sleep until my body wakes up naturally. I write six hours a day. My writing room is filled with natural sunlight. I socialize with accomplished writers,'" Katherine announced proudly.

"Yes, yes. Exactly. When you say these out loud you can actually see yourself writing, can't you?" Jenny asked.

"Actually, I can. I can see it's possible, but I don't know *how* I can make it possible." Katherine was beginning to feel disillusioned.

"Ah, stop yourself right there," Jenny blurted. "Just stay with me a little longer here. Now, I need to tell you a very important piece of information, and I need 100 percent of your attention."

Katherine quickly snapped back to the present moment, pen poised, ready to record the lesson. "Ready," she confirmed.

"You don't need to know *how* you are going to achieve a goal. Your job is to know what it is that you want and to visualize that in your mind every day, while feeling the emotions of living that life. Then all you need to do is take action. Take any action in the direction of that goal and experience the 'magic' of the Law of Attraction."

"Magic?" Katherine questioned. It had all been sounding pretty logical up until this point.

"Yes, it's like magic, and this is the coolest part about this law. You see, once you can clearly see and feel your new life and you start some action creating momentum in that direction, then you give the Universe or God or Source, whatever you choose to believe, the opportunity to do its job. That is to provide you with the people, ideas, opportunities and resources you need to achieve your goal. See, you need to be the same energy or vibration of what you want first, and you achieve this by keeping this picture in your mind and taking action towards your goal. That brings me to the third type of affirmation, action affirmations. Like I just said you don't need to know the whole plan, you just need to take the first steps."

Katherine was fascinated with the logic and simplicity of this lesson. "I totally understand, and this makes complete sense," she marveled.

"Okay then, show me how you understand. What action affirmations would you write for becoming a successful writer?" Jenny asked.

"Easy. I purchase books on how to write. I read one of these books a week. I research support groups for writers. I join one of these groups. I write *anything* for an hour each day." She looked at Jenny with confidence. "How's that for starters?"

Jenny grinned from ear to ear. "You'll be joining us on our yearly vacations very soon!"

"Heck, yeah!" Katherine agreed.

"The fourth type of affirmation is your 'why' affirmations. Why do you want to write? Do you want to do this to make your family proud? Do you want to feel proud of yourself?

Do you want to make a difference in the world, or do you just want the feeling of accomplishing something outside of that comfort zone of yours?"

"Let's see," Katherine said. "Um, all of the above?"

They both laughed. Katherine felt she was progressing quickly, and she thought Jenny did too.

"So what's the last type of affirmation?"

"The last type is easy for you because you have already figured it out. It is the thoughts you need to think to achieve your goals. Remember how you identified the thoughts you didn't want the other night and then rewrote them as the thoughts you did want?"

"Of course."

"When you add these to your list of affirmations, you spend time each day visualizing yourself with these new thoughts and thinking this new way, which positively affects your life and the goals you are striving to achieve. It also reminds you that you have decided to think differently and specifically about your new thoughts. You now have a powerful list of affirmations that clearly describes what you want and why you will achieve it. The list reminds you of the thoughts and actions you will take and paints a picture of your new, fabulous life. Each day when you read this list, you can close your eyes and easily see and feel what it's like to have this scenario as your new reality."

"Wow! I can see how this works now. My only concern is the fact that I find it hard to see anything in my mind. I mean, even when I had renovations done in the restaurant and I could see the drawings from the designer, I still couldn't see how it would look until it was actually finished. Are you sure that just reading this list will do the trick for me?" Katherine didn't want to voice her "but." She sincerely hoped Jenny had a solution for her.

"There are a couple of tricks I use that can make this list more effective for you," Jenny assured her. "The first trick is to add photos to your affirmations, to create a vision board. When you combine an affirmation with a picture that illustrates or enhances that affirmation, it gives your mind an image to start from and build upon. Just grab a scrapbook or corkboard, cut some photos out of magazines or use your own photos, then print out your affirmations and stick them together like a collage. This will definitely help with the visualization part.

"The other trick I use is music. It is just as important to feel the emotions of living this life as it is to see it in your mind. Choose a song that really inspires you, something that you really love, and then play it when you are looking at your goals and visualizing this new life. Remember our theme song for our trip to Italy that year? It was 'Tonight's Gonna Be a Good Night'?"

"Yeah, I remember." Katherine smiled.

"How do you feel every time you hear that song?" Jenny asked.

"I feel pumped. I feel happy. I feel excited and anticipate good times ahead." Katherine felt energized just talking about it.

"Wouldn't you like to have similar feelings when you visualize your goals? You want to choose a song that makes you feel amazing when you hear it, and then you can associate those incredible feelings with your new life. Talk about turbocharging your affirmations! This little secret will get things happening faster than you ever thought possible," Jenny said.

Katherine's head was starting to spin. "This is just awesome, Jenny. I am feeling so thrilled right now. I can actually see how this would work. I can't wait to complete this list and get some photos together. I am starting to see myself as a writer for the first time! What else do I need to know?"

"I think that's enough for today." Jenny laughed. "Just by going through this exercise and creating the habit of focusing on your list and doing something each day to move you closer to your goal puts you ahead of most of the population. Rome wasn't built in a day. I don't want to overwhelm you with too much information straight off the bat."

"Okay, but can we organize a time for us to get together again once I have my list done?" Katherine wanted to keep this momentum going, plus she wanted Jenny to keep her accountable.

"Of course! It's Friday today, let's meet for lunch next Friday."

For the first time that she could remember, Katherine felt optimistic and hopeful. She loved having an adventure that was about to be set in motion. The flash of the big picture came flooding in that moment, and it felt right.

Go Inside the Chapter:

— Do you find yourself "wanting" something in a particular area of your life, but never getting it?

— Have you tried using the Law of Attraction in the past with only mediocre results?

Scan the code below or go to **www.niywd.com/chp4** to access a free bonus video with author Natalie Ledwell.

Inside, Natalie reveals the important piece of the success puzzle that Katherine misses in Chapter 4 – something that many of us overlook *even though it's right in front of us.*

You'll also discover Natalie's easy seven-step formula to activating the full power of the Law of Attraction, so that you can start attracting more abundance into your life almost immediately!

CHAPTER FIVE

Don't Wait for the Ducks, They'll Never Line Up Anyway

That night after dinner with Jenny, Katherine was wide awake. Writing her list of affirmations came easily. She had been thinking about what she *really* wanted since Jenny stumped her with that question at lunch several days earlier. After only 20 minutes, she had a healthy list of affirmations describing the life of a successful writer.

I am a successful writer.
Writing flows easily and effortlessly for me.
My writing is inspiring to many.
I feel completely fulfilled when I write.
My writing changes lives.
I win awards for my writing.
I sleep until my body wakes up naturally.
I write six hours a day.
My writing room is filled with natural sunlight.
I socialize with accomplished writers.

I purchase books on how to write.
I read one of these books a week.

I research and join support groups for writers.
I write anything for an hour each day.
I make my family proud.
I am proud of myself.
I make a difference.
I am worthy of success.

❧

Katherine suddenly felt inspired to write affirmations about other areas of her life: painting a picture of fun, leisure, challenge, excitement, and love.

I am in a loving, fulfilling relationship.
I am the perfect mate for my perfect mate.
I allow love to find me.
I attract the love I give.
I accept social invitations.
I am open and ready for a loving relationship.
I am 145 pounds.
I am energetic.
I am fit and strong.
I am in control of my health.

I am trim, taut, and terrific.
I respect my body.
My partner loves my body.
I always make healthy choices.

I am motivated to exercise each day.
I nourish my mind, body, and soul.
My body is beautiful.
I have $100,000 in savings.
I have a manageable balance on my credit cards.
I travel to London, Paris, and Nice.
I have more money than I need.
I am grateful for riches in my life.
I am wealthier each day.
I pay my bills easily.
Money flows to me freely.
I allow money into my life.
I choose an abundant life.

As she scanned these lists, she noticed one glaring omission. There was not one affirmation about the restaurant. It dawned on Katherine that even though she had decided to "stay and be happy" for now, it was not what she ultimately wanted. Remembering how important it was not to include the actual words of the things she didn't want, like "stress" and "debt," she decided that omitting the restaurant was a great idea. *I'll just focus on what I do want and trust that the universe will keep up its end of the bargain,* she thought.

It seemed silly to just think about this, but she couldn't deny the success of her friends. She had set her intention and promised Jenny that she would achieve her goal, regardless of the cost. It was just going to take some getting used to, that's all.

Katherine typed her affirmations, changed the text to a larger font, and printed them out. She cut up the paper and spread the pieces across her desk.

She pulled out magazines, looked up quotes that matched her new beliefs, and found pictures of people she admired. She cut out image after image that represented what she wanted in her life. Famous writers. Exotic locations. Trim, fit women. Stacks of dollar bills. Fireworks. Images suggesting love and creativity. Everything that made her feel that rush of exuberant passion, she cut out and placed under the affirmations on her desk. When she was finished, she stood back to drink in the picture of the perfect life that she had illustrated through these words and photos.

What a mess, she thought. *There is no order here. What am I supposed to focus on first?* Looking at her horizontal collage, she tried to visualize her new future. *Maybe I'm just tired*, she thought. *I'm not getting anything from this. I'll try again in the morning.*

As Katherine awoke that morning, she remembered the creation strewn across her desk. No *organization*, was her repeating thought. She then started to mentally organize her photos and affirmations. She began creating a mental slideshow, combining each group of affirmations that related to each goal. She could see the affirmations on the actual photo that she chose to reiterate that affirmation. Like a virtual filing system, she could see these slides flipping over steadily in an orderly fashion. *That's better*, she thought. Her eyes shot open with sharp realization, "That's it!" she said. "I should create a slideshow, and I can add my music to it as well!"

Katherine jumped out of bed and started scanning each photo. Using software she found online, she created a slide show of affirmations, photos, and music. She watched it over and over again. As the feelings of abundance filled every part of her, she took out her laptop and opened it up. She thought about her affirmation to "Write anything for an hour per day," and she just started writing. Perhaps it was due to the fact she had just watched her personal "mind movie," but she started writing a movie scene that outlandishly depicted her on the most popular talk show in the country.

SETTING: Stage of the Diane Craven show. Katherine Murray sits in elegant attire just across from the notable correspondent.

DIANE

We're here talking with writer, Katherine Murray, whose book has become the biggest hit in publishing history. It was created from a transcript she wrote in record time. Welcome, Katherine. (The audience gives a standing ovation for the writer/creator.)

The scenes went on to show Katherine in countless news articles for the outrageous contributions she had made to the world. Then, there were the scenes of love. SETTING: Beautiful, huge kitchen. Sleek, black wood cabinets. Elegant, marble countertops. Katherine walks in to find a handsome man awaiting her.

MAN

Hi, beautiful. Welcome home.

He comes to her and wraps his arms around her. She feels warmth, passion, and love.

❦

Katherine wrote scene after scene. Some were long and detailed, and some were short yet poignant. Sometimes she wrote stories. Sometimes she wrote articles. Most times, though, she wrote about how she imagined life would turn out for her. These scenes were for her eyes only and extremely cathartic. Some were of situations she wanted to create and others were pure fantasy. All were happy, positive scenes in which the main character triumphed over hardship, helped others and lived a lavish, fulfilling life.

Some days she stayed awake until four o'clock in the morning and wrote and wrote. She started realizing all that she really wanted from life. Things she felt guilty for wanting or she thought weren't important enough or realistic enough. The more she wrote about these positive scenarios, the more she believed they could become part of her reality. The scenes became easier to write as writing revealed itself as her passion. She assumed love wasn't an option without ever asking herself why she thought this was so. But it didn't mean that it wasn't what she ultimately wanted.

She wanted love, she wanted wealth, and she wanted a feeling of purpose. The more she gave to others, the better she felt. The more little successes she achieved, the more she wanted to give. She was ready for more, and she was ready to let go of the belief that she should feel guilty for wanting more.

❦

An announcement came over a megaphone requesting that Katherine and Rita Lopez of "Live with Rita" return to the set. Katherine tousled her hair in the mirror of the bathroom, smiling fondly at the memory of Jenny and the night she had first shared her secrets to success that catapulted her into living the dream.

When they returned to the interview, Katherine shared her same memories with Rita. It was clear that Rita connected.

"I compared the scenes I wrote when I first started to what I write now. In the beginning, they all revolved around my getting out of a bad situation, which my friend and mentor, Jenny, pointed out. I wasn't looking beyond that. I wanted to go beyond just getting by, because, ultimately, I wanted money! I wanted the freedom and security money could provide. I wanted to be successful! I wanted to make a difference." She looked out to the audience and thought about her home and the backyard she'd always dreamed of and the big beautiful pool that always looked so peaceful and inviting. She thought of the times when everything seemed to be working out, until something else would pop up.

Katherine looked back at Rita. "And I also wanted love. And it's okay to want all of that. It's not okay to have guilt about wanting it."

"Okay, I've gotta ask... how did you get everything you wanted?

"Well, I started first by becoming clear about what I wanted, focusing on that every day, and taking some small action steps in the direction of my goals."

"So you focused on being an award-winning scriptwriter?" Rita asked.

"No, actually I didn't, and that is why I was able to become one." Katherine replied.

The puzzled look on Rita's face made Katherine giggle. "I'm sorry, Katherine, but you're going to have to explain that," Rita said.

Katherine described the lunches she would have weekly with Jenny and the revelation that dared her to think big. "Jenny explained that I didn't need to know how I was going to accomplish something, so in the beginning I just focused on being a writer but I didn't specify *what* I was writing. I trusted that I didn't need to see the whole plan and have my ducks all in a row. As long as I held up my end of the deal, visualizing my goal of writing as if it existed already and taking some action in that direction, the universe would hold up its end of the deal by transpiring to make sure that I had the ideas, people, and opportunities I needed to complete the job."

Rita's expression had changed from bewilderment to confusion.

"I can see by the look on your face that this sounds as strange to you now as it did to me the first time," Katherine explained "But, there is a very logical, scientific explanation as to why this works."

"Yes, I could do with a logical, scientific explanation right now, and I'm sure our viewers would too," Rita said.

"Well, it involves the Reticular Activating System, or RAS for short. This is a bundle of neural fibers at the base of the brain. The RAS plays a role in several of the body's functions such as breathing, sleeping, and the beating of the heart. But in this application, it functions as the gatekeeper of thoughts that are delivered to the conscious mind from the subconscious mind."

"Okay, this is sounding very scientific right now," Rita quipped.

"It's okay, it's not too complicated. Let me explain it like this: Our conscious mind, which is the one where we are aware of our thoughts, processes around 40 bits of data per second, or thereabouts, depending on which scientific source you reference. The subconscious mind, which actually controls our thoughts and actions 90 percent of the time, processes around forty million bits of data per second, again, depending on your source. The numbers may change but the ratio is always similar."

"Whoa," Rita said, shaking her head.

"I know, right? Can you imagine being aware of 40 million bits of data per second? You would be insane! So thank goodness for the RAS."

"But, what 40 thoughts does the RAS choose out of that forty million?" Rita asked and leaned forward on her chair.

"Great question!" Katherine was feeding off Rita's energy. "Most of the time we don't even contemplate this and our subconscious works automatically off old, programmed thoughts that play like a CD stuck on repeat. Not that all programming in there is bad. But let me ask you something, Rita. Have you ever been sitting at a set of traffic lights and realized that you don't remember actually driving for the last ten minutes?"

"Umm, yes, and on more than one occasion," Rita replied sheepishly.

"Don't be ashamed of this, we all do it. It's a perfect example of subconscious programming. Remember how hard it was to learn how to drive? Having to consciously remember about the mirrors, the gearshift, the indicators, what direction you had to drive, and, of course, all the other drivers on the road? It was nerve racking."

Rita nodded.

"Well, through repetition over the years, we no longer have to consciously think so hard about the mechanics of driving, and that's why you can totally be unaware while you are behind the wheel and not have an accident. Your subconscious mind is running the show."

"Fascinating," remarked Rita. "But, what has this got to do with the thoughts the Reticular Activating System chooses?"

"Well, through repetition, just like driving the car, we can program the RAS to filter through the thoughts we *do* want and the things that are of most interest to us- those things that will help us achieve our goals."

"Right." Katherine could see Rita didn't quite comprehend the enormity of this lesson yet.

"Let me give you an example. When I was in the market for a new car, I explained to my girlfriend, Allana, that I would ideally like a small car that was a hardtop convertible because I lived in the city and was concerned about vandals slashing a soft-top car. Allana suggested that I consider the Volkswagen EOS. I was familiar with the VW Golf, which was out of my price range then, but I had never seen or heard of the EOS. So that night, I went home and looked for this car online, and it was exactly what I was looking for. The next day, I was driving around, and lo and behold, I noticed four EOS cars driving past me. Had an EOS driven past me before? Probably, yes. Why hadn't I noticed these cars before? Basically, they weren't of interest to me before, so my RAS didn't send that information through to my conscious mind."

"Oh!" Rita looked as if she was trying to process this information overload.

"So, by focusing on your end result every day, through repetition you are programming your RAS and telling it, 'These things are of interest to me. If you see anything within the forty million bits of data per second you ingest that can help me achieve my goals, make sure you shoot it straight through to my conscious mind so I am *aware* of the ideas, people, and opportunities the universe is sending my way.'" Katherine always came alive when she talked about this subject. Watching someone like Rita Lopez come to the realization that she had more control over her life than she knew up until that point was unbelievably rewarding.

"That is incredible," Rita gasped. "But, wait a minute, you said that you *weren't* focusing on being an award-winning script writer."

"Very perceptive," Katherine said. "In the beginning, I just focused on being a writer because when I spent time writing, I felt alive, and I thought that if I could make a living at something that made me feel so good, it wouldn't even feel like work. My friend Jenny taught me that I didn't need to know *how* I was going to achieve that. But what I came to realize was that I couldn't be married to *how* it was going to happen."

"Okay, I am officially confused," joked Rita.

"To be honest with you," Katherine said, "in the beginning, I couldn't see what becoming a writer looked like, and I didn't really care. I just wanted to write. When I started to visualize what that would look like, I imagined myself writing books, hanging out with groups of other writers, and spending months working in a beautiful, sunlit room. So at first, I thought that's the way writing would manifest itself in my life.

"When you think about it, writing could take any form—books, blogs, and journalism for newspapers, magazines—anything. At the time, I was writing for at least an hour a day. Some days I would write short stories and some days I would write mock-up articles describing the future success I was going to have. Most of the time, I was writing movie scenes about the positive outcomes I was going to achieve. It was easier for me to see and believe these situations if I saw them as a movie scene with different characters. And I would be able to describe the scenery, the action, and the responses.

This helped me visualize these positive outcomes in my mind more easily. They were personal and only meant for me."

Rita was leaning so far forward, staring intently at Katherine, that Katherine thought she might tip out of her chair.

"Then one day, I was sitting at my computer marveling at how happy I was and comparing that to how miserable I was before I started applying Jenny's wisdom to my life. I remember thinking that *everyone* should know about this stuff. Jenny referred me to many books. Some were written as long ago as the early 1900s. So, why didn't everyone know this? My life had completely changed from this information, and I wanted to shout it from the rooftops. I wanted to find a way to spread this message and get the word out so people could realize that they don't need to suffer and feel miserable anymore. I wanted people to know that they had control over the direction of their lives and that they could have anything they wanted. That's when I got the calling."

"The calling?" Rita asked.

"Yes, I call it the calling. I looked back at my computer screen to the movie scene I had just completed, and I *knew* I had to write a movie that would teach people the skills that enabled me to create the life I wanted. Now, you have to appreciate the fact that I didn't know how to write a movie script. The pieces I wrote were like therapy for me and not professionally written at all. The more I thought about this completely crazy idea, the more I could see it unfold as a reality before my eyes. The storyline, the lessons, the characters, the scenes. I could see it clearly in my mind and knew, without a doubt that I must write this script.

"The excitement and pure faith I had when I thought about it overshadowed any illogical thought, doubt, or craziness. Logically, it didn't make sense, but I knew it had to be done.

It took a while before I actually was able to sell the restaurant and have the opportunity to sit down and write uninterrupted, but as you know, when I did finally sit down to write the script, it just poured out of me within a week. If you had said to me a month, even a week before I wrote the script that it was going to become an award-winning hit movie, I would have laughed my head off. There was no way that would ever happen. But I knew I wanted to be a writer. I knew I wanted to contribute and help other people, so I kept my focus on that goal and stayed open to the possibilities. Even though I thought I would be writing books, the universe inspired me to write a movie instead.

"When I think about it, every time I reflect on how I will achieve a certain goal, in the end, I never end up accomplishing it in the same way that I expected. If I had forced myself to write a book and didn't listen to the message the universe was sending me, I don't know if it would have been as easy to write or to achieve success as a writer using the path given to me. I trusted that the *how* was not my job. I just needed to focus on the *what*."

The din of the applause was deafening. Katherine was welling up with tears of joy, witnessing the complete understanding of not only Rita Lopez, but of the entire studio audience. This was her inspiration and her vindication that following such a crazy idea was absolutely the right thing to do. She hoped that in this past hour she was able to express this message in a way that would open the minds and possibilities for everyone who watched it.

Go Inside the Chapter:

— Have you had trouble reaching a particular goal in the past, even though you pushed really hard to achieve it?

— Do you ever feel frustrated when you work hard and still don't see the results you were expecting?

Scan the code below or go to **www.niywd.com/chp5** to access a free bonus video with author Natalie Ledwell.

Inside, Natalie walks you through the "Aha! moment" Katherine experiences in Chapter 5, when she realized that putting less effort into her goals would actually get her more results. (Are you pushing harder than you should too?)

Natalie also shares with you her little-known secret to going from struggle and strife to effortless success!

CHAPTER SIX

So What Do You Stand For?

It was early one afternoon and Katherine was in the restaurant completing one of the homework assignments Jenny had given her when Ryan strolled through the door.

"Hi, Ryan! Hey, do you think I'm adventurous?" she asked.

"Umm, I suppose you could be, given the right set of circumstances. Why do you ask?" Ryan seemed puzzled.

"I'm just going through one of the exercises my friend Jenny gave me to do."

"Really? Let me have a look. What have you got there?" Ryan stepped around the desk to peer over Katherine's shoulder. He and the whole team had noticed the improvement in Katherine's attitude since she'd been having those weekly lunches with her girlfriend, and he wondered what sort of lunch led to homework.

"The exercise will help me figure out who I am and what I stand for. Basically, I'm trying to find the core traits that I place the highest value on." Katherine pointed to the paper in front of her. "She's given me a list to prompt me into identifying what is most important to me."

Ryan scanned the page in front of them. It listed different attributes in alphabetical order: *Adventure, Accomplishment, Balance, Confidence, Control, Drive, Empathy, Freedom, Friendliness, Growth, Honesty, Integrity;* there were so many.

"Well, you are definitely honest and loyal," Ryan offered.

"Yes, I know that. So are you, by the way." Katherine smiled at Ryan. "I suppose that's why we get along so well. We both value those traits and appreciate them in each other." Katherine paused for moment. "You know, I don't say this often enough, but I really respect you and appreciate your skill and talent. You are the reason the restaurant does as well as it does. You are a great leader, and the staff really loves you and looks up to you. You clearly have a passion for creating incredible dishes, and people keep coming back for your amazing food."

"I suppose you can add 'sincerity' to your list." Ryan blushed. "So, what's the purpose of this exercise?"

"Well, according to Jenny, when you know what you value most in the different areas of your life, and you intrinsically know who you are in any situation, you can make the right decisions faster and easier every time."

"That sounds like an interesting concept," Ryan mused. "What exactly does she mean?"

"Well, the example she gave me was choosing a career. She is in a mastermind group with a woman called Carmen, who used to be a doctor. Carmen told Jenny that when she looked at all her doctor friends who loved being doctors and loved the medical profession, they all had similar core values. They all had drive and a deep devotion to medicine. They were in control, showed discipline, had the ability to focus on the illness, and the self-control to emotionally distance themselves from the patient so that they could treat the condition in the best possible way. Plus, they enjoyed the wealth that came with their position.

"When Carmen completed this exercise, she understood why she was feeling so disillusioned with her life. She realized that she had become a doctor to help people, not to make money. She was empathetic bordering on sympathetic, so she was constantly getting emotionally involved with her patients, which was taking a heavy toll on her. She was friendly, honest, spontaneous, loving, and open, and she rated herself very high on integrity.

"She started to notice a correlation between the drugs prescribed to patients and their specific side effects. She also started to realize the direct link between happiness levels and health levels. It got to the point where she couldn't in all honesty keep prescribing the drugs that she believed made people sick. Now she uses her knowledge and experience to heal people naturally through her suggestions of maintaining a healthy lifestyle and mental practices, *and* she absolutely loves what she's doing. Carmen confided in Jenny that had she identified her core values before entering the medical field, she would have realized it wasn't the profession for her."

"Wow. Imagine wasting all that time on a career you don't even end up enjoying!" Ryan said.

"Well, when you think about it, it wasn't a complete waste of time. As Carmen pointed out, if it hadn't been for her experience with medicine, she wouldn't have had the perspective, the unique approach, and the health results she is achieving for her patients now. It's kind of like it was a necessary stepping stone. She had to experience that so she could be the amazing healer that she is today." Katherine admired the courage Carmen showed by walking away from a coveted career like medicine to stay true to her values and follow her passion, and she shared this with Ryan.

"Yes, I suppose that's true," Ryan agreed. "So, what do you think your values are besides being adventurous?"

"Well, if I were to describe myself in a perfect situation..." Katherine became self-conscious but forced herself to talk. "I would say that I'm creative, impulsive, honest, loyal, a free spirit at heart, adventurous, and have a passion for helping other people." Once she opened her mouth, it came out freely. It occurred to Katherine that these were the qualities of a successful writer. "Not that I feel I've been showing those qualities much lately. I seem to be too influenced by stress and responsibility for the true me to come out. What about you, Ryan? What do you think your core values are?"

"Hmmm," Ryan ran his eyes up and down the list in front of him. "I would say that I'm driven, a decision maker, a leader, creative, loyal, and a team player. I'm honest, and I have confidence and control. I take action, plus I have the ability to see the big picture and all aspects of a business, and... I make it happen."

"Yes, I can see that about you." Katherine leaned back on her chair to look closer at him. "I think you just described the perfect business owner right there. I wish *I* had some of those qualities." No sooner had the words come out of her mouth that both Katherine and Ryan silently acknowledged to themselves that she was not meant to be operating a restaurant.

"Come on! You're a great boss," Ryan blurted out, hoping to break the uncomfortable pause in conversation.

"Thanks, Ryan. That's a very nice thing to say, but between you and me, we both know that this is probably not my ideal career." It was becoming more evident each moment that Katherine had to get away from the restaurant business. It was sucking the life out of her, and she clearly wasn't being true to herself by staying. "But you would be a great boss. Have you ever thought of owning your own restaurant?"

"Maybe the thought has crossed my mind once or twice." Ryan grinned. He told Katherine that he thought about having his own business almost every day. He told her about the innovative menus he would create using fresh vegetables and herbs he grew in his garden at home. When he interacted with the staff he would act as if they were his team.

"Well, enough idle chit chat for now, I have a kitchen to prepare." With that, Ryan quickly disappeared into the kitchen, whistling a joyful tune.

Later that evening, Katherine was curled up on her couch in her most comfortable pair of PJs, sipping a piping hot cup of peppermint tea. Normally her tea would have been a large glass of cabernet, but part of her new health regime was to eliminate her consumption of alcohol during the week. She was continuing with her homework and identifying her core values for another life area—relationships.

Let's see, she thought. *What are my relationship core values?* She remembered saying to Ryan earlier that day that "in a perfect situation" she would have the opportunity for the real Katherine to come out. It had been several years since the breakup of her marriage, and it pained her to think about it. Who she was at the beginning of that relationship and who she ended up being at the end were completely different people.

"Come on, Katherine, you can do this," she rallied herself. She started to think about the type of relationship she wanted and how that related to her core values. Looking at the list she had written earlier that day, she could see how several of them applied to a relationship situation. "Impulsive, a free spirit at heart, adventurous, honest, loyal." The last two values reminded her how her ex-husband had been anything but honest and loyal. Momentarily, she felt the crushing betrayal of his indiscretion with a 25-year-old and cringed.

Loving, she thought, trying to change the subject in her mind. *Passionate, thoughtful, considerate, and supportive.* These were all qualities she wished her ex had had, but unfortunately his qualities were more self-serving. As she looked at her list of values for "Relationship Katherine," she realized these were the same values she hoped her perfect partner would possess. Then the penny dropped. *Well, if this is what I want to attract, then I better write it down and focus.*

I attract my perfect partner.

He is loving, considerate, and supportive.

He loves being adventurous with me.

We are passionate together.

Just writing these affirmations and adding them to her list made Katherine excited at the prospect of meeting her perfect man, and she knew she would easily recognize him when he came along.

A few afternoons later, Katherine was in the middle of paying bills to all of her vendors, which she hadn't been able to successfully do for months. While it felt good to have these bills paid and to be making an actual profit, she still lacked the enthusiasm for the restaurant that she felt when she wrote her scenes. The difference now was that she knew this business wasn't meeting her basic values, which was why she wasn't fulfilled.

As soon as she thought about changing lives by telling stories, she lit up. In a weird way, it made her happy in her current position. She knew where she was going, and it was the passion that kept her going each day.

"Here," Ryan said excitedly, slapping a packet onto Katherine's desk.

Even though she was engrossed in accounting, Katherine was still taking part in her fantasy life. The slam of Ryan's papers and his instant towering over her startled her.

"Um, what's this?" Katherine snapped back, looking at the papers.

"My offer," Ryan said with complete confidence.

Katherine started to fear the worst. She recalled the conversation they had the other afternoon and started to question if she had said something wrong. She thought they had shared a rare, lovely moment together, but maybe she had interpreted it all wrong? He must have seen right through her. He knew she wasn't meant for this business, and now he wanted to jump ship. She shouldn't have confessed that she wasn't meant for this business.

She started mentally beating herself up as only she could do best. *Great! Abandon me now. I may as well give this restaurant away to any schmuck who wants to take it off my hands. Who would want it now? I may as well shut the doors tonight and walk away because without Ryan this restaurant is nothing.* Her mind was racing headfirst down a rabbit hole of negativity. Ryan had a very determined look on his face, and she reacted to his strong front. "Offer to leave? You want to leave?"

Ryan shook his head, "No, Katherine. This is an offer to buy the restaurant. Come on! Are you really surprised after our conversation? I thought it was pretty obvious."

After comparing their respective core value lists, Katherine did think that the best person to run the business was obvious, but she wasn't quite expecting this.

"Look, Katherine, deciding that I would like to buy this restaurant was a huge decision for me and a major commitment. However, your friend Jenny was right, it was an easy one. You know, I have been entertaining the dream of owning my own place for a while now, and after that little exercise the other day, it hit me that I was born to do this. Everything I value and stand for is suited to this business, and I know I will be a great restaurateur.

"That night, I discussed my idea and told my wife, Marie, about that exercise and my list of core values, and she agreed whole-heartedly that I should go for it. I went to the bank the next day, and I have enough equity in my house to take out a second mortgage. You helped me realize that this is absolutely the right move to make, I just know it." Ryan was speaking with such conviction that little bits of spit flew from his mouth and landed on Katherine's desk.

He paused for a moment, leaned forward, and lowered his voice, "Just like you know you should be writing."

Katherine gulped. His enthusiasm was infectious, and she knew he was right. How could Ryan afford to pay what she would ask for? How would he even know what she would ask?

"Just look at it and get back to me by the end of the week." He headed toward the door, turned, winked at her, and walked out after his final word, leaving Katherine dumbfounded.

As soon as he left, Katherine stood up to close the door to her office. When she returned to her desk, she sat down and looked at the neatly stacked papers that Ryan had had professionally bound. She didn't know what to do. The obvious answer was to open it and read it, but she felt frightened. Here she was being faced with something she had asked for, but the proposition represented so much change that it scared her senseless. There would be no more excuses, no more reasons for not following her dream.

A few deep breaths later, Katherine dragged the packet closer. She looked to the door to confirm that she had privacy. She turned to the first page and then the next. She kept reading and reading and reading.

After turning the last page, Katherine smiled. In a matter of moments, an afternoon that seemed so typical turned into the answer she'd been asking for. Ryan was the perfect person to acquire her business, and he had been right under her nose the whole time. In fact, there was no one else she would rather sell it to. His plans for the business resonated with everything that she believed. His passion for food and his lust for the business matched the same feelings Katherine had for her new venture, and it was clear as day. It didn't take Katherine a day or night to mull over the contract. As soon as she turned the final page of this agreement, she knew she was in.

Katherine came out of her office, her face broadcasting sheer relief and happiness. She looked to Ryan immediately. He had a knowing smile. He knew she wanted out as much as he wanted in.

In two days' time, the deal was signed, sealed, and delivered to Katherine's attorney. She was really free to follow her new passion and the feeling was indescribable.

Go Inside the Chapter:

— Are you ever frozen with indecision when it comes time to make an important decision?

— Do you stress or worry over decisions you've already made?

Scan the code below or go to **www.niywd.com/chp6** to access a free bonus video with author Natalie Ledwell.

Inside, you'll discover how Katherine overcomes 'analysis paralysis' in Chapter 6 and makes a clear, empowering decision that takes her to the next level in life… and how you can follow in her footsteps.

Plus, you'll learn Natalie's secret to making clear, confident decisions in life quickly, easily and without stress!

CHAPTER SEVEN

Negative People: Can't Live With Them...

Those first few days of freedom were exhilarating. It was the weekend and for the first time in years she didn't have to shove down some food and get dressed up at four o'clock in the afternoon, preparing for the night's work ahead. It was Saturday night and for once she didn't have to be anywhere. Katherine celebrated the best way she could imagine. She changed into her pajamas, grabbed a tub of Ben and Jerry's ice cream, watched a string of movies she had been promising to see for several months, and passed out on the couch in a sugar coma. Pure bliss. Sunday morning she woke by nine o'clock and couldn't wait to visit the local Farmer's Market. She had wanted to go to visit it for years, but she never woke up in time after a late night's work. As she walked through the market, Katherine felt an overwhelming wave of gratitude and appreciation not only for the wonderful aromas and flavors of local produce but also for the feeling that she was part of the human race once more—that life was a wonderful experience again.

Come Monday morning, there was a drive inside Katherine once she reconnected with her "calling." Even though this newfound freedom caused her to feel some trepidation, she realized she'd made the right decision and that she could overcome any limiting belief or other obstacle that held her back. But it didn't mean that these limiting beliefs ceased to challenge her. As soon as the excitement began to flow, and she knew where she was going and what was in store, a moment of doubt would set in. This wasn't uncommon. After all, she was still human. She was a woman in her forties, just now realizing that she could pursue a dream. Yet in demanding times, some questions still disturbed her.

While writing was something that she wanted to do and felt compelled to do, she knew very little about scriptwriting. There was a lot of learning involved in writing a screenplay, and she didn't have the appropriate script software, education, or tools she assumed were necessary. Even if she did have these, she wouldn't know how to use them. Did she need to know how to network with certain people? Should she be reading certain books? Would the industry think she was too old?

There were so many factors involved that seemed beyond her reach. She questioned her abilities, her presence, her experience, and whether she could actually achieve this dream.

"You're doing it again!" she said to herself while looking in the mirror. The negative thoughts and the doubts came rushing back like a bad smell. It was a cycle, a pattern she would still need to break through and reformat. She was her own challenge, and her only answer was to surmount it by writing another script that aligned her with the right vibrations of success. She accepted that doubts would come, but more importantly, they didn't stop her because she knew now how to move forward. This felt so right. She came alive. This was her passion.

The impetus to learn about scriptwriting became so important and critical to Katherine that she knew she would get past the doubt. She knew that the only way to keep the doubt at bay and let her true self shine was to remind herself of where she was going and who she truly was.

Jenny had prompted her to change her restrictive thoughts. That night, she created a slide show on her computer to add to the visualizations in her mind and the daily writings she had begun. When she had written daily about fixing the restaurant business and feeling good about it, this became her reality. Now she would need to have the same visualization about this next stage in her life.

She started her morning by watching the slide show she made. The pictures that echoed her success and feeling of constant profusion brought her further away from any sense of doubt and grounded her steadfast in her purpose. On top of that, she created an affirmative pronouncement that would counter every thought that resisted her goals. If her mind told her she was too old, she negated it with an affirmation of youthful energy. When her mind questioned her abilities to learn at an accelerated speed, she refused it with the undeniable gift of learning and intelligence. She quickly dissolved every thought that threatened her aspirations with irrefutable assurance, diffusing the uncertainty with positivity.

The opposition to any doubt became so strong that it took Katherine just one night to learn all she needed to begin her journey as a screenwriter. She learned the format, the purpose of a scene, the story as a whole, the timing, the dialogue, and the basics of writing and creating a film. Katherine mastered how to download and use scriptwriting software and how to determine where each plot point needed to go, and she was ready to write her first scene as an educated screenwriter. To begin, she wrote a montage accounting the series of achievements that she expected would soon follow.

(MONTAGE: High-energy MUSIC plays.)

INT. Katherine's bedroom. Evening.
Katherine sits at her desk and reads a book on
screenwriting. Books half open with the pages
folded lie next to her. Books with titles like *Producing Your
First Film, The Art of Making Movies,
Write a Screenplay in 30 Days*, and *How to Sell Your
Screenplay*. Her eyes absorb an open book with complete
intention.

INT. Katherine's bedroom. (cont'd)
Katherine is holding another book, reading it as
she eats a piece of toast.

INT. Katherine's bedroom. (cont'd)
She finishes the last page of a book. She puts it
down and picks up another.

INT. Kitchen. Evening.
Katherine grabs milk from the fridge and pours it into her
teacup. She sits at the kitchen table with her laptop open.

INT. Kitchen. (cont'd)
Katherine pulls out Scriptware software and puts it into
her computer. She starts to write. Her fingers are fast and
determined. She barely stops to take a sip from the teacup.
She continues to type.

INT. Kitchen. (cont'd)
Still typing. She smiles.

INT. Kitchen. (cont'd)
Still typing furiously. She laughs.

INT. Kitchen. (cont'd)
She nods her head in pleasure.

INT. Kitchen. Morning.
Katherine walks in, still in her pajamas. She sits down.
The typing continues. It's faster than before.

INT. Kitchen. Morning.
She walks in. She's wearing jeans now and a tee
shirt. It's a new day. She sits down again with a steaming
teacup and begins to type.

INT. Kitchen. Evening.
Katherine leans back in her chair. She wears a
huge grin.

INT. Kitchen. (cont'd)
She collects a big stack of papers from the printer.
She piles it on the table and clips it together.

CLOSE UP: The first page of the stack reads
Write Here, Write Now
A Screenplay
By
Katherine Murray

∾

On the set with Kirk Browning, the morning show correspondent of the popular *Wake Up with Kirk* morning show, Katherine was remembering what she wrote in the script when Kirk cut in. "The question everyone is dying to know is: How did you write such a powerful script from concept to completion in just one week?"

"I didn't know I could do it that fast. I knew that I wanted to learn how to do it fast. But the actual conception of the story and completion of it? I didn't know I was capable of doing that until it actually happened. But I will tell you that the vibrations I felt inside were similar to those I felt when I completed it." She shifted in her seat, wondering if she was making sense to Kirk, and if she would make sense to the viewers. "I had to start by writing for myself. I created a montage scene, where I was absorbing all of the best material. I wrote it in a montage sequence to give myself the picture of effortlessly learning fast in an enjoyable, fun way. I then envisioned and wrote myself finishing the script, not knowing the time span, but just knowing that I wanted to finish. When I was done, I was filled with complete contentment and passion." Katherine felt she was reliving the moment as she spoke of it.

"What did that feel like?" Kirk, taking notice of her changed demeanor, joined her in that reverie.

"I could feel the high-energy flow of production as if I was writing the screenplay right then and there, and the creativity was pouring out of me like a water fountain turned on at full force."

"And, how long after did you actually write the screenplay?"

"Two days after that scene, I sat down at my computer for one week. I left only to get food, go the bathroom, and change my clothes, which I did twice. At the end of the week, it was complete." The room was silent. The crew and Kirk seemed amazed. Katherine still felt a rush of fulfillment thinking back to the moment when she was happily done and completely satisfied with her efforts.

But it wasn't so easy to achieve this feeling. Just after she completed the script, she felt as if she'd conquered the world. It was the perfect prelude to visiting her family and celebrating her father's birthday. On the drive down the coast to where they would meet, Katherine couldn't stop visualizing the effects the film would have. She was even blowing herself out of the water with what she'd accomplished in such a short period of time. She couldn't remember the last time she'd felt so proud of herself.

"What are you going to do for money?" her sister asked in the middle of lunch on the first day.

She cleared her throat and said, "Well, I've got a bit from the sale of the business, and soon enough, I'll make money from the film."

Katherine could remember it vividly. She sat at the table with her five sisters, two brothers, mother, father, cousins, aunts, and uncles. It was a large family gathering, and somehow, she landed as the central topic of conversation.

"But darling, you know nothing of the film industry, and you can't write," her mother laughed as if this was an adorable dream for a child but hardly realistic for a grown woman.

They all laughed at her as if she were absurd.

"It's a relentless business! Don't come asking us to lend you money!" Her sister's husband, Tomas, chimed in. It was the most humiliating experience she'd felt in a long time. Absolutely no one in her family took her seriously. As she was walking down the hallway she heard one of her sisters talking to her brother Ken in her old childhood bedroom. "Katherine has completely lost it this time. I mean, a screenwriter? How

could she possibly think she could pull this off? It's the craziest thing I've ever heard."

Katherine didn't expect her family and friends to understand. To an outsider it *was* a crazy idea. She had no experience, no track record, and no knowledge of the industry.

What she did have was happiness. Writing was her passion, and it fulfilled every part of who she was. "Time will tell," she told herself.

✑

Later that evening, Katherine opted to take a walk after dinner. She remained silent for most of the gathering and ignored the stares and questioning from her supposed supporters. It was all coming back to her. That voice that she'd worked so hard to silence was louder than ever. Was this a ridiculous endeavor? Did she make a big mistake selling a business that was starting to provide for her? Was she a complete idiot going into a business she knew nothing about? Just because she wrote something didn't mean that anyone would think it was of any value. Maybe her family was right. But at least she could be sure about one thing: She couldn't deny feeling so alive when she wrote. Writing was in alignment with everything she believed and stood for.

The sun was just setting despite the late hour, and Katherine realized she was exhausted from the negative thoughts. She saw a small bench and collapsed on it, not acknowledging the older gentleman sitting right next to her.

"Just beautiful, isn't it?" the man said, with the most gentle, positive voice she'd heard all day. She nodded in agreement and let out a quiet, "Uh, huh."

"It's easy to feel gratitude when you can enjoy such an incredible view," he continued.

Katherine hadn't even noticed the beauty around her or where she had ended up. As soon as he brought her attention to it, she looked up and around. Somehow, she had walked up to a beautiful mountain view of the ocean. It was all consuming. Her personal mantra rang out in her head, "I choose to be happy." She didn't have to focus on the negative things they were saying to her. If she did, she would end up right back where she started. Instead, she had to turn her attention to the beauty around her. That's when she could shine.

Despite her realization, she must have still held a distressed look on her face. "How's your day going?" The man asked in a tone that suggested he thought that something might be wrong.

"Is it that obvious?" She laughed and he joined her. "Well, I had a pretty challenging day with my family. Let's just say they're not on the same page as I am."

He didn't ask why. Instead he replied with more laughter. "You know, if I had listened to my family, I would have never become a *New York Times* bestselling author!"

"Really?" Katherine couldn't help but feel relieved to hear this. She still wasn't sure why, though. She still felt that her family's opinion should matter to her even if it was different. She searched the man's face looking to see if she recognized him as someone famous. He did look vaguely familiar.

"Look, most people are decent and they try to do their best with what they have. They're not always going to understand you or even want to. That's just the truth. You just can't let the negative thoughts influence your positive thoughts," the man told Katherine.

"How do you do that, though?" she questioned.

"Instead of getting angry or blaming them, just love them from a distance. Wish them well and give them as much of your wisdom and positivity as you can without taking it away from yourself. In their own way they mean well. So trust that and focus on yourself. No matter what they think, your success will greatly influence them. So whatever prevents them from being on the same page as you... who cares?!" Katherine smiled at the man. It was the happiest she had felt all day. He was right. She knew she was on the right track, and it annoyed her that she kept falling victim to her family's opinion and her own inner doubts and demons. "So, *New York Times* bestseller eh? Any title I would know?"

"Maybe a couple." He smiled. *"Between a Rock and a Hard Place?"*

Katherine gasped. "Darren McQueen?" He smiled and nodded.

Darren McQueen was the number one bestselling author of thriller spy novels. He was a celebrity! Katherine could hardly believe that she was sitting next to him on this random bench in her hometown.

"Oh my goodness. What are you doing here?"

"I have friends who live here, and I love the peace and quiet."

"I'm getting life advice from Darren McQueen," Katherine said disbelievingly, acting like a starstruck teenager.

"Honey," he continued, "I'm going to leave you with one piece of advice that I wish someone had given me when I was rising to the top. Be the example, the benchmark. Let people see you do it so they can believe they can do it too. You have no idea how your actions can cause a ripple effect of positivity. And please," he looked deep into her eyes, "don't worry about your family, because those who have it in them to change will come to you."

~

"When we return, Katherine will tell us about the phone call that changed everything. And still to come, Katherine answers your questions," Kirk spoke as he slowly walked alongside the pool with cameramen walking backward to capture him and his neatly folded hands. No one could tell that Kirk was reading the teleprompter in front of him; it was routine to him. He smiled warmly and finished, "We'll be right back."

Katherine watched from afar as Kirk was being filmed. She could barely contain her excitement, knowing that her taping would air. With each show, she was reminded of her tremendous capabilities and gratitude.

She knew at this point what she and Kirk would be discussing when the cameras started rolling again inside. She remembered it all too clearly. But before that moment and even after that moment, there were challenges. What she learned from these experiences would be forever valuable.

Go Inside the Chapter:

— Do you believe it when the people around you tell you that you can't do something?

— Do you really take what other people think about you to heart?

Scan the code below or go to **www.niywd.com/chp7** to access a free bonus video with author Natalie Ledwell.

Inside, Natalie walks you through the steps Katherine follows in Chapter 7 to finally bust through her comfort zone, escape the influence of negative people and go for her dreams.

Plus, Natalie reveals how you can safeguard yourself from the negative influence of others, so that you can move faster and easier towards your most inspiring goals!

CHAPTER EIGHT

Those New Thoughts Look Fabulous On You!

"There are no studios that are interested in my script," she remembered telling Jenny at one of their lunches. "I've been literally knocked back by 10 studios so far, and I know they are not even reading the script. They call me too quickly with an apology. I just need one studio to sign me. I'm feeling frustrated and helpless all over again. I had no idea how difficult this would be. And my self-esteem? Every rejection feels like a personal stab into my heart!"

Jenny just looked at Katherine with a blank stare. "Well, aren't you going to say anything?" Katherine asked. Finally Jenny broke her silence. "Can you hear yourself?"

"Well, I can! But can you? You're just staring at me like I'm a lunatic, which is what I feel like." It was obvious Katherine's adrenaline was pumping.

"Well then, I guess that's what you are."

Katherine was about ready to stand up and leave. She wasn't getting the sympathy she wanted. Just as she was about to leave money for her share of the bill, she took a deep breath and it all began to sink in. She sat back down and nodded her head. "Oh, I get it now. You're teaching something to me, right."

"The universe is always listening," Jenny said. "Okay, what do you mean?"

"There are no studios interested in your script? You wish just one studio would sign you?" Jenny asked.

"Is that wrong?" Katherine was confused. "I thought I was supposed to ask for what I want."

"Wishing isn't really asking. It's kind of like being passive aggressive with the universe. If you really want it, just focus on your end result and leave the *how* up to the universe. Stop saying that no one is interested. You're trying to force the situation. The universe will hear that and guess what? It will give you more studios who aren't interested."

"But I need to take some action. Shouldn't I be approaching these studios?"

"Of course you should be, but remember you have to be flexible and open to other opportunities to get your movie made, and you won't come across them if you're sitting on your butt at home. Kath, what you've been doing is great. Really it is. Look how far it's gotten you. I know you want more. It's easy to apply the Law of Attraction, the LOA, when everything is going smoothly, but it's times like these when you really need to apply the principles. That's the difference between successful people and those who aren't successful. For successful people, this is just part of the process, water off a duck's back. Because successful people are always striving for a new goal they understand how important it is to enjoy the journey, the process. They know that each rejection is a learning curve and one step closer to their goal. So start talking to me about how once studios read this, they are going to fall in love with it. Or, tell me that no matter what, this film is going to happen."

"Think about the language you are using and please, Katherine, change your perception to something positive. Don't assume that it's all negative. Maybe these studios weren't the right fit. Do you really want the producers of *Nightmare on Elm Street* to make this film?" Jenny paused for another moment while Katherine absorbed the new way of looking at things that she was describing. "These aren't 10 rejections. They're 10 reasons why they aren't the right studios for the film. They are 10 steps closer to the right one. Here, let's play a little game."

"Here we go," Katherine moaned.

"Now don't be like that," Jenny scolded. "I'm trying to help you here. One of the habits you can adopt that really helps to positively activate LOA is for you to 'talk as if' and 'act as if' your goal is a reality right now. So, tell me, what does your day look like today now that your movie has been a great success?"

"Well, I'm not hanging out in this shopping center food court with you," she started. "We're having lunch at Claude's on the Marina. I'm wearing that beautiful Gucci dress we just saw and those hot pink suede Jimmy Choo's. I have a meeting this afternoon with a studio exec to discuss my next project."

"Yes," Jenny chimed in. "You don't know if you'll work with him or not. After all, since you won an Academy Award you can pick and choose who you work with."

"That's right! I have a special cabinet in my writing room in my five-bedroom waterfront home that not only has my Oscar and my Golden Globe but also has plenty of space for more awards. Oh, and I'm packing later to fly to London to be on a talk show over there. I'm terribly in demand these days." Both Katherine and Jenny giggled to each other.

"So Kath, how do you feel when we talk about how wonderful it will be as if it's already happening? Can you nearly taste it? Can you feel how possible this is and how great life will be when you get there? Don't you just believe it's already done?" Jenny asked while smiling.

"How did you get to be so smart, Jen?" Katherine felt euphoric, like she was vibrating at a higher level.

"Years of practice," she smiled. "By role playing like that, talking and thinking like your movie is a huge success, actually makes you a vibrational match to that life. It builds your belief, it keeps you focused on the end result so the universe can step up and start making things happen. Now, you said something interesting before about travel. It is very probable that when your movie is a hit you will have to do a press junket to promote it, right?"

"Absolutely," agreed Katherine.

"Okay, so let's think about how you can act as if your movie is a massive success. Is your passport current? Do you have a couple of plain, good-quality suits for your interviews? Is that the hairstyle you want the world to see? The camera puts on five pounds; are you happy with your weight for TV?"

"Good points," Katherine nodded. "My passport will be up for renewal soon, so I'll fix that, and I have been thinking about a classier, more modern haircut. I am on a great health regime at the moment, so I'm already taking action on my weight."

"Ahh, but now your motivation, your why, when you exercise and make healthy food choices from now on will be so that you look great on your press junket. Again, it's another little trick to keep you focused on the end result and to not get hung up on how it will unfold for you," Jenny clarified.

"Oh my god!" Katherine gasped suddenly changing the subject. A portly woman walking past their table had completely distracted her. "Check out the muffin top on the woman coming our way. Look Jen, at your two o'clock. Does she not have friends or a mirror? How could she leave the house looking like that? Snap." Katherine laughed as she looked to Jenny to join her in this light-hearted moment.

Jenny stared back at her like she was looking at a misbehaving teenager.

"This is exactly what I'm talking about! Kath, you just finished telling me that you're not happy with your body. Has it occurred to you that maybe you're attracting your condition with your thoughts?"

"Come on, Jen, it's funny! We're not hurting her; she can't hear us. It's just a little joke between the two of us." Katherine couldn't understand why Jenny was being so judgmental.

"No Kath, you don't realize that you're just hurting yourself," Jenny said, shaking her head with disappointment. "Every time you think those things about another person, every time you say something nasty or *funny* about another person, every time you judge another person, the universe hears you and you just attract more of it back to yourself.

Think about it, how many times a day do you make these observations about other people's bodies?"

It was like Katherine had the wind kicked out of her. "Oh my God. I am bringing this all on myself. *I'm* the one being judgmental." When she really thought about it, Katherine was exhausted with the amount of thought energy she wasted each day, mentally beating herself up over her frumpy stature and picking other women's bodies to pieces. She was disappointed in herself.

"Look, don't be so hard on yourself," Jenny reassured her. "We all get caught up in juicy gossip and these types of conversations from time to time. Now that you're aware of how powerful your thoughts and words can be, just make a pact with yourself to cut back on the cynicism, okay?"

"Sure," Katherine said sheepishly. "Can you help me, too? Pull me up when you hear me trash talking anyone?"

"Absolutely." Jenny grabbed Katherine's hand and gave it a supportive squeeze.

Katherine felt immensely grateful for Jenny's friendship and her simple, commonsense advice. She felt a little embarrassed now that she realized how easily she could have avoided this whole panic attack and frustration. If she were going to succeed, she would need to shed these old ways of assuming the worst, and judging others unnecessarily. This new realization would bring her closer to what she wanted. With this new perception, she could build a Teflon shield against the studio rejections and against virtually any person who said no.

She was already writing these scripted scenes and making mind movies that depicted her submitting her screenplay to multiple sources and networking with the right people so that she would get noticed along with the screenplay. They also illustrated the actual film, what it would look like and how people would respond. They also detailed what her life looked like now that she was a success. It was a part of her daily routine to revisit these scenes, visualizations, and movies that she was making. She knew there was more she could do, though. Through Jenny, she became deeply engaged with the Law of Attraction and how every thought and belief was determining her actions and how everything needed to be in play for LOA to work. This powerful revelation became more evident during the past months. Jenny even had her on a daily regimen that would continue to support her new beliefs and action.

Jenny had Katherine take a few moments every day to role-play and really focus on what it was that she desired without any obstacles. Instead of wondering if it were possible, they would talk as if the movie were already a success. Jenny told her to also write it out until she could feel it, as if it were here now, right now.

Jenny then asked her to continue creating and watching movies that reflected what she really wanted. She encouraged her to keep making the movies that she could play for her mind to watch every morning and every evening so she could easily visualize this as her new reality. Jenny told her to include every detail that matched her dream to make the movies more effective. If a discouraging moment surfaced, Katherine was told to watch a movie that instantly made her feel empowered again. These movies were to contain the affirmations that fortified the new beliefs. Not only would she watch the images but she would also see the language that would speak to her subconscious mind. It was the language that supported the images and would add force to her new beliefs. She asked that Katherine spend at least fifteen to twenty minutes a day reaffirming these new beliefs.

Jenny worked with Katherine to establish new positive habits in place of the negative habits and encouraged her to do little things every day in preparation for the success about to befall her. She reminded her each time they spoke that there was an infinite amount of happiness in the universe for the taking.

It became a daily habit for Katherine to sit at her computer and find the images that would illustrate her desired outcome. She would write an affirmation, just one line that clearly stated her vision.

I write an amazing screenplay.

The movie earns an Academy Award.

The movie gets made in alignment with the message.

The movie creates a ripple effect of positivity throughout the world.

Millions of lives are changed for the better.

She continued to write the affirmations. In just minutes, she would fashion a short movie with inspiring music representing what she wanted to accomplish. She would play the movie for her mind to see multiple times a day.

Each movie reminded her and instilled the vibrations related to the feelings of the success she desired. The more she did it, the more permanent her inner confidence became. None of the movies, however, introduced the barriers that were to come.

Before the phone call that changed everything, Katherine submitted her script to every agent, manager, and producer who she saw fit. She researched the right prospective people she believed could make her screenplay into a movie. She attended every local event she could get into that would bring her closer to the people who could assist her in the production. She taught herself the proper terminology and process of producing a film so that she appeared to be knowledgeable in this part of the business.

But the reception was not as she had hoped. Most looked at her as the unripe newcomer that she was. If they hadn't heard of her and were not introduced to her by someone of credibility, her words weren't heard. She told this much to Jenny over one of their bimonthly lunch dates.

"I've been really focusing on the positive, Jenny. Really, I have. But it's just not going the way I planned."

"That's not how it works, Katherine. In fact, most of the time, it never works out how you planned. But, that's okay. In fact, it's better," Jenny said.

"How so?"

"Because it brings you closer to what you really want. You think one way is the only way, but it just isn't. The universe has a funny way of bringing you what you asked for in a way you never thought possible."

"How can I get my film made without a studio taking it on?" Katherine asked her wise friend.

"Make it yourself." Jenny seemed to have the answer to everything. Katherine never thought about making a film herself. Though she had educated herself on the development and the course of such a production, she knew that she would need help actually making the film. On top of that, the funding would be more than she could afford at the moment.

"I just don't have the money right now, or the resources. Ideally, the right person falls in love with the idea and we go from there. But it doesn't seem to be panning out that way," Katherine responded.

"Katherine, you wrote it in one week. It's only been a month since you started making submissions. I know you're eager, but while you wait, maybe there's something else you could be doing," Jenny suggested.

"Oh yeah? Like what?" Katherine ears and eyes were wide open.

"You write scenes everyday, and I've seen those movies you make for yourself. You make them in no time. Why don't you—"

Katherine interrupted, "Make a movie trailer myself!"

"Make a movie trailer yourself," Jenny finished in agreement, but with less inflection as Katherine. "If you want these people to understand the notion of the movie and the effect it's going to have, why don't you create it in a short, compelling preview? Get them wanting more."

"It's brilliant!" Katherine could barely contain herself.

"And look, my nephew Larry is in film school. His focus is cinematography. I'll give him a call. I'm almost certain that he'll be interested in helping with the filming. It'll make for good demo material for his resume. He'll recruit some actors from the school, and we'll make a coming attraction of the screenplay." Jenny was getting excited, too.

"Why didn't I think of this sooner?" Katherine questioned with a thrill in her voice.

"Again Katherine, it has only been a month. I wouldn't say you're falling behind in the least."

Katherine laughed. She went home later that afternoon to write the scenes that would represent the movie. She pulled pieces from the screenplay that invoked inspiration and created what she felt was the perfect representation of her screenplay and vision.

In the following weeks, she was resolute to bring this vision to culmination. Though Jenny's nephew Larry, the technical crew, the actors, and the other participants were eager to partake in the production of the trailer, problems still surfaced. People showed up late to call times. Actors had outlandish requests that stalled production. Faulty equipment snatched more money out of Katherine's pocket, and the mood quickly drifted from energized to aggravated.

But with all of the challenges, Katherine could feel the frustration, but it wasn't consuming her like it did in the past. As she reflected on each trying situation that arose, she became more conscious of its purpose. Very rarely would achievements in life be accomplished through a path of no conflict. Like a child learning to take its first steps, Katherine was bound to fall from time to time. The more daring the goal, the more likely the sweat. It was becoming clearer to Katherine that this was part of the pleasure, part of the fulfillment.

She found herself enjoying the obstacles and, even more so, the emotion that came from pushing through and succeeding with each one. It was the same thing Jenny had taught her.

She was reprogramming her mind in these very experiences. Her thoughts and behavior were changing. The more these situations surfaced, the more natural it was for her to apply a LOA principle to it, and the more practice she acquired. She kept remembering a quote she had once read: "Nothing has meaning other than the meaning we give it." Every time a difficult situation arose, she chose to see it as a lesson and a challenge. There was always a solution, and each solution taught her more about herself and the industry she was becoming a part of.

The end vision of each goal was magnificent, and her determination was so high that she began reaching goals. The diversions along the way were just that, a detour from the planned path. She simply had to be flexible and open to taking alternate routes to get to where she was going, and each new road paved a new lesson for her. These unexpected conduits were welcome.

As her research made her more skillful at directing and producing, she knew just how to pull these people together so that she had the team that would get the job done. That's exactly what she did. She did what was necessary. She said no to the preposterous requests from actors, and she sent the latecomers home and sought out others who respected the opportunity. Within a few weeks, she had a three-minute preview that exemplified everything she wanted the movie to be.

It was the perfect practice for when she would create the film. Every time she thought, *During production, I'll do it this way instead*, it built her belief that creating the film was inevitable.

She was right.

Go Inside the Chapter:

— Do you find it hard to stay motivated and on track with your goals?

— Do you have difficulty dealing with stress during times of hardship?

Scan the code below or go to **www.niywd.com/chp8** to access a free bonus video with author Natalie Ledwell.

Inside, Natalie pulls back the curtain on how Katherine injects more fun and joy into pursuing for her goals in Chapter 8. You'll discover how you too can enjoy the journey of going for your dreams instead of just desperately yearning for the end destination.

Plus, you'll discover how to reconnect with the "great big why" behind your goals, which will reignite your passion and motivation to keep moving forward *even when the going gets tough!*

CHAPTER NINE

You Don't Have to Do It All by Yourself

"We're back with Katherine Murray, creator and writer of *Write Here, Write Now,* who has invited us here to share her story." Narelle Gallway, an esteemed *60 Minutes* reporter, turned away from the camera and back to Katherine. They had cordoned off a section of the pool area at a five-star hotel in Nice, where Katherine was taking a short break from the hectic schedule she had been subjected to. So much for her short break. "We left off with you writing the film in just one week. You experienced some rejection along the way as you submitted the film. You then made your own preview for the script to show its potential to film producers and agents. What happened after that?"

"The phone call." Katherine beamed.

"And, what was that call?"

"It went something like this, 'Hello, Miss Murray. This is Jeffrey calling from Fox Studio. We've received your tape and screenplay, and the studio is very interested. Can you please return the call to set up a meeting?'" Katherine recited.

"You submitted the preview to how many people before receiving this phone call?"

"I submitted it to a combination of 250 studios, managers, producers—anyone I saw as potential," Katherine recalled.

"And only one called," Narelle confirmed.

"That's right. Only one called. I received two more calls months later, but we were already in production at that time."

"And, as the story goes, once you started production, it was completed within six months and released shortly after?"

"Correct."

"And, here we are sitting at this stunning five-star hotel in Nice, France, with an award-winning creator and writer. Your first screenplay, your first film, and two Academy Awards, one for each nomination." Narelle paused, allowing time for the viewers to react. "How does that feel?"

Katherine shook her head for a moment, and then said, "Narelle, It feels awesome! You make it sound so clinical and easy. But, it wasn't a slam dunk."

"Really? Why not?" Narelle asked.

"Well before getting that call, my financial situation had become dire. I had sold the restaurant, but after paying off all of my debts, it only afforded me enough money to make my preview film and to pay my bills for a short period of time. It got to a point where I wasn't sure how I would be able to pay for my mortgage, my cell phone, or even my next meal." Narelle sighed and nodded.

"Did you have family to help or support you?"

Katherine laughed at Narelle's question and was immediately brought back to this desperate time. She did have the support of her friends, especially Jenny. But her family's stance on this issue was loud and clear. Without even trying, she could hear their voices in her head. "Don't come asking us for money," she could hear her brother-in-law, Tomas, repeating. She didn't blame them for thinking this. She had borrowed so much money in the past, and she truly felt a weight lift when she could finally pay them back after the sale of the restaurant. She didn't even bother asking the question. She knew the answer would be no.

"What was your master plan, Katherine? Walk up to a studio and have them welcome you with open arms?" Her sister taunted. At the time, she couldn't help but ask herself the same question. Was this all wrong? Was she doing something far too audacious? She put in the effort and took action, but maybe this wasn't what she was meant to do. Wouldn't it have fallen into place by now? She had come so far, but it was a dark moment indeed when she started to seriously consider taking a job somewhere and putting her dream on hold.

Back at the makeshift set, Katherine continued to share her experience with Narelle.

"So, other than a few close girlfriends, most people thought you were crazy, and some even tried to talk you out of your dream, despite your promise to yourself to not let them influence you. That must have been very challenging," Narelle observed.

"Negativity will always be a challenge. It's how you deal with it and what you do with it that's the difference between people who get to live their dream and those who just keep on dreaming."

"And how do you deal with that? What do you do when you feel like you are alone?" Narelle asked.

Katherine smiled instantly. "You always have all the support you'll ever need and you're never alone."

"Never?"

Katherine leaned in to Narelle. She gestured to the trees around them. "It's easy to feel like you are alone and that no one supports you. But that's precisely the time to connect with something outside of yourself. Something that is pure love and encompasses everything that is."

"What do you mean by that?" Narelle asked.

"When you can experience being connected to what I like to call Source, then you never feel lonely. Instead, you feel peaceful and supported by the Universe. There is nothing lonely about it. See, I came to realize that there was a certain level of success I could achieve on my own, through my actions, forcing situations to happen. If I wanted to achieve audacious goals and dreams like writing an award-winning script, I had to trust in a power greater than me. I had to acknowledge its existence and purposely be grateful for it each day. I had to allow it to create the circumstances I needed to reach my goal, and I had to trust that when these opportunities presented themselves to me, they would steer me on the right path."

"Wow, you know I never looked at it that way before. So you're talking about trusting in God?" Narelle questioned.

"Yes, God is one word you can use to describe this power. It goes by many names: God, Buddha, Allah, Source, the Universe. You will use the word that means most to you. It's the utter faith in its existence that makes you appreciate the redness of a rose or the beauty of a sunset or the smell of fresh-cut grass. The belief in this energy is what makes life magical and wonderful. Trusting in it gives you all the support you need." Katherine knew this was a difficult thing to grasp and hoped the viewers of the show would understand.

"I understand what you mean. But I'm sure many people are wondering how they can do this. I mean, as simple as it sounds to be connected to Source, I think people have a hard time knowing how to do that," Narelle said.

"Of course! I had to teach myself how to be connected. But I did it, and there are many ways to do it."

"Please share with us!"

"First," Katherine looked into the camera. "Don't worry! You don't have to turn into a deep-breathing yogi to be connected spiritually. It's whatever works for you to feel connected to the greater level of consciousness."

"So meditating, for example. Is that necessary?" Narelle asked.

"Meditating is amazing. I love to meditate. But it's not the only way. Many people get scared about meditation and what it means. I like to think of it as putting the world on pause. Giving your subconscious and super conscious mind a state of peace. I practice this daily."

"Really?"

"You can meditate anywhere, especially in nature. In fact, one of my favorite ways to connect with Source is to simply walk along my property and take in the nature around me."

"So this isn't something you only do when challenges arise? This is something you do every day?"

Katherine laughed. "Challenges happen all the time. That's just life. But, meditating daily brings me into a state of allowing. In this state, my mind is clear and able to do what it does best. This is how I attract the people, places, and events needed to work out the best situation for me to achieve my goals. When I look back on how my life was unfolding, I realized that all the planning in the world could not have created the chain of events that ended up making my film the worldwide smash hit that it is."

"And, this is why things played out the way they did and you ended up here?"

"That's right. You know, I had a dark moment the day I realized not one person was saying yes to even looking at my script. I went to all the effort of creating a preview of it, but nothing was happening. Or so I thought. I was about to apply for jobs. I even considered applying on a studio lot just so I could be in the environment. That was when I received an instant message on Skype from my friend. She insisted that I come with her to some party. I really didn't want to go, but then I remembered something my friend Jenny had said."

"What was that?" Narelle asked.

"She said I had no more business hanging out in my comfort zone and that when something feels uncomfortable, I should do it."

"And so, you went?"

Katherine smiled. She remembered getting ready that night and going a little more out of her way than she normally would to cheer herself up. She took out her best dress and designer shoes. She wore her favorite and most expensive jewelry, and she did her hair differently.

When she walked into the party that night, she knew she looked amazing. She was determined to have a great time despite the day she'd had. Everyone turned when she walked into the room. There was an air of confidence about her that captured everyone. It especially captured one man.

"Well, either everyone is going to keep staring or someone is going to have the nerve to come up to you. I'm typically not shy. So here I am. I'm Glen. What's your name?" He was masculine and handsome, and Katherine felt immediately charmed by him.

"I'm Katherine."

"Hello Katherine. What brings you here?"

"A friend of mine knows the host."

"Oh really? And who is this friend?" Glen asked. Katherine could detect some flirtation in his manner.

"Leanne. Do you know her?"

"Leanne is my friend. I know her quite well."

"Well, she is a friend of the host, and she demanded that I come. Though I haven't met the host yet!" Katherine laughed at the irony.

"Sure you have!" Glen announced.

"I have?"

"You're looking right at him." Glen smiled.

Katherine looked around only just now realizing the beauty of the home she was standing in. Pictures of Glen with celebrities and political figures adorned the walls. "What is it that you do, Glen?"

"Oh, you know... stuff."

Katherine giggled. "Oh, you're going to be that way, are you?"

"More importantly, what do you do?"

At this point, Katherine felt embarrassed. Here she was looking like a million bucks yet she couldn't scrape two pennies together. The reality was that after this party, she would go back to the job board and start searching for her next paycheck-to-paycheck job. "I'm sort of between jobs right now."

"Really? So you're going to be like that are you?"

The rest of the night went famously well. Katherine felt a kind of excitement that she hadn't felt in a very long time. The conversation flowed so easily in fact that she hardly finished two glasses of wine all night. She was very happy

Leanne had invited her to the party and that she met such an interesting man. She was still floating on cloud nine when he called the very next morning.

"Hey Katherine, it's Glen. I normally wait two days to call, but that rule seems to be dying, so what do you say we get a coffee this morning?" Katherine loved his assertiveness and agreed before he finished the question. Something told her to go right away.

An hour later, the two of them were sitting outside a cute cottage-style restaurant with a cappuccino and a café au lait.

"So, come on, you have to tell me a little more about yourself. I mean the mystery can only go so far."

Katherine felt that uncomfortable feeling again, so she went with it. "Well, to be honest, I just sold a restaurant that I wasn't passionate about. Turns out I am passionate about writing. Something I really knew nothing about. But I wrote a screenplay in a week, just filmed a preview of it, and now I'm trying to figure out plan B since none of the studios I submitted it to are interested." She smiled. "There, how's that?"

"Fantastic!" Glen threw his hands up. "Even more fantastic is that you wrote it in a week!"

"Yep."

"Well then. I think it's fair enough for me to tell you what I do."

"Please do," Katherine said, feeling off the hook now and ready for another sip of her drink.

"I help people like you get their movies made."

Katherine laughed. "Right!" She didn't believe him for a second.

"I'm not joking."

Something about his serious face told that her he wasn't. The realization that he might be serious made Katherine shift in her seat. "Are you like a producer or something?" she asked.

"You could say that. The real deal is that studios pass on some of the best movies. I like to take the movies that don't have a shot and give them life. While it might not be the traditional route, often enough it's better than the studio route."

This was starting to sound like music to Katherine's ears.

⁓∾

"So you meet this guy Glen, and he helps you make your movie? What happened with Fox?" Narelle asked.

"Jeffrey from Fox called the day after I met with Glen. Both had very generous offers, but it seemed that going with Fox would be a more reliable decision."

"So you went with Fox after all? Did production on the film go smoothly?"

Katherine immediately responded, "I'm so happy to say, that it did not go smoothly. If I thought creating the preview was a fight, the tension we hit making the film was a rollercoaster. But it was a rollercoaster I loved riding."

Katherine was on a fast and exciting ride. In the mornings before she arrived on set, she practiced her meditation and affirmations. She felt enthusiasm at the beginning of each day. She had never felt so motivated. She was even making special requests to the universe through specific visualizations.

❧

(MONTAGE: Soulful music plays.)

EXT. Outdoor café. Evening.
Katherine sits across from a Man at a bistro-type table. She is smiling. Her eyes are sparkling. She tilts her head in a flirtatious manner.

EXT. Outdoor café. (cont'd)
Katherine is laughing with the same handsome man. He grabs Katherine's hands and both of their expressions soften as they gaze into each other's eyes.

EXT. Park. Day.
Katherine and the Man ride bicycles alongside each other. She cuts him off, and he laughs.

INT. Theatre.
Katherine and the Man sit together, their arms wrapped in each other. They laugh together.

INT. Katherine's family room. Evening.
Katherine reads a book and looks up to find the Man standing with ice cream, a movie, and a smile.

EXT. Mountains. Day.
Katherine and Man dressed in outdoor trekking clothes are hiking up a big hill. She pulls him up behind her.

EXT. Wilderness.

Katherine is standing and kneeling below her is the Man with a ring.

∾

"I honestly feel like everything always works out for me now," Katherine told Glen one evening at dinner. They were spending more and more time together, and it seemed effortless for Katherine. Glen, while disappointed in her decision, supported her journey with the other studio. They became fast friends. He showed up almost everyday to cheer her on. She felt good about herself. She was fitting into clothes she hadn't worn since she was 20. The best part of it was that she didn't feel like she was making a monumental effort. It all just started happening so easily.

"It does seem that way," he smiled while pouring her a glass of wine.

"It's like the restaurant and all that struggling are from another life," she paused for a moment and looked at Glen. "And, of course, meeting you."

He smiled in response. "What about meeting me?"

"I've never met anyone quite like you. All I know is that I feel really good when I am with you."

"Katherine, I hope I've shown you that I think the world of you. I want to support you in every way. Come on, though—"

"What?" she asked.

Glen looked so deeply into her eyes that she thought she was going to melt. "This isn't just a friendship anymore."

That night, Katherine and Glen grew closer than she'd ever felt with anyone. It was clear that she had found the perfect partner she'd always wished for, only this time she didn't have to wish. She asked and he appeared like a gift from the universe.

Go Inside the Chapter:

— Do you generally feel connected to your inner guidance system—your intuition—or cut off from it?

— Do you sometimes take action that you know deep down inside is against your gut instinct, only to regret it later?

Scan the code below or go to **www.niywd.com/chp9** to access a free bonus video with author Natalie Ledwell.

Inside, Natalie offers you a deeper look at why "trust" and "letting go" are the secrets that allow Katherine to accelerate towards her end goal in Chapter 9, and how you can duplicate her success.

You'll also learn several easy, fun ways to strengthen your "inner guidance system" so that you can use it to know exactly what actions to take to bring you more happiness, joy and fulfillment in any situation!

CHAPTER TEN

How Many Ways Can You Skin a Cat?

Katherine remembered how excited and enthusiastic she was the first month arriving at the set. The moments after her first meeting with the studio had her soaring higher than cloud nine. She was high, and she was witnessing her dreams come true. Everything she'd ever hoped for became a reality and she drank in every wondrous moment of it. Her relationship with Glen was blossoming. Her relationship with her family was the best it had ever been. It was like everything was falling into place for Katherine, and she gratefully acknowledged the flow she was in. By the second month of production, cracks had begun to form and the proverbial wheel was falling off. She found herself questioning the veracity of the film in its final state and whether Fox was the right decision after all.

Enthusiasm started turning into head-butting frustration. Ron Calais was the Fox-appointed director, and if he and Katherine shared any common ground in relation to the movie, it resembled a small tuft of grass.

Ron was constantly trying to steer the film in more "commercial" directions that didn't hold true to the integrity of her intention. He was a company man, and he knew this is what Fox wanted. Katherine knew that she would have to fight a little harder to maintain the authenticity of the message she was on a mission to share. Ron wasn't her only problem. The project was being funded out of pockets other than her own, and the low budget that had been allocated was proving to be troublesome to the final product.

The production was not going smoothly for Katherine, and she was disappointed more than once. Her only saving grace was Executive Producer Baxter Barnes and, of course, her biggest cheerleader, Glen.

"Come on Katherine, spit it out," Glen jeered at her. "We're in this beautiful restaurant looking over the water, we have a superb meal, I'm looking at the most gorgeous woman on the planet and she's staring at her plate playing food hockey with her brussel sprouts. What's going on in that pretty little head of yours?"

"I don't want to bring you down with my problems," Katherine sighed.

"Well princess, you are bringing me down by not telling me your problems right now, so spill the beans."

Katherine reluctantly lifted her head and looked into Glen's iridescent blue eyes. "It's just that nothing is going according to plan. I should be happier than a bird eating a french fry right now, but Ron Calais is making my life miserable. It's like he doesn't get the message at all, and the movie he wants to make is just hideous. I'm trying to stay positive but I feel like I'm walking through wet cement, and every inch I gain completely takes it out of me. Seriously, this is not what I visualized at all," she vented.

Glen reached for her hand across the table and looked compassionately into her eyes. "You'll get through this, baby. I know Jenny is giving you some advice. What does she say?"

"As usual, Jenny has been great," Katherine started. "She has me doing a bunch of stuff that really has been helping me stay positive even though everything around me seems to be going to pot. Of course, I'm still doing the basic things like staying focused on my end result and spending time every day visualizing and feeling the emotions of seeing the movie I want to make being a massive hit. She also suggested I collect social proof to confirm that this has been done before. She said it will help me to believe that I can do it too. So I've been reading some amazing biographies of inspiring moviemakers, like Quentin Tarantino, Robert Rodriguez, Peter Jackson, and David Lynch. Their stories are so inspiring, and they have overcome much bigger obstacles than I'm facing right now."

"She's a clever cookie, that Jenny," Glen said. "Not just a pretty face." He was trying to lighten the mood a little.

"Yes, I'm very fortunate to have her as a friend. She also gave me this awesome exercise to do for when things are starting to spiral downward. You see, misery loves company, and one negative thought leads to another. Next thing you know your whole day is one negative black hole. You just want a do-over and and to start all over again. So, before I get to that stage and I realize the day is heading in the wrong direction, I simply walk away and reboot."

"Reboot?"

"Yeah, I interrupt the pattern. I walk out and grab a coffee and walk in nature. I head for the dog beach and watch happy puppies frolicking without a care in the world. I meditate. I jump in the car, turn the radio up really loud and sing at the top of my voice. Sometimes I call Jenny, and we have one of our little role-plays that we do, talking about the movie already being a hit. I just remove myself from the negative energy, and do anything else that gets me back into a state of happiness. This way, I have blocked the negative energy from ruining the rest of my day. Unfortunately, my little reboot exercise didn't work so well today, and Ron Calais has become the bane of my existence." She was tired of talking about it and reliving her day all over.

"Well, there is one piece of advice that Jenny hasn't told you yet," Glen offered.

"Really?" Katherine said, incredulously.

"You could ask for help." Glen pointed to himself. "I have a little bit of experience in this area, you know."

"Thank you for offering, Glen, but this is something I need to do for myself. We are still in the beginning stages of our relationship, and I don't want to stuff things up between us by bringing work and possible artistic differences into this amazing thing we have going on here. You understand, don't you?" Katherine was hoping that statement wouldn't upset Glen and affect their incredible relationship.

"Okay, I get it. You want some independence, and you don't need me telling you what to do. Don't worry, I'm not that egotistical," he joked. "If you would prefer not to get help from me, what about Baxter Barnes? He likes you, and he seems to hold a similar vision about the film. I'm sure he would be able to offer some great advice."

"Great suggestion, honey. I'll go see him tomorrow." Katherine was feeling relieved and instantly began enjoying her evening.

The next day, production started smoothly, but by lunchtime Ron was starting to bark ridiculous directions to the crew, and Katherine had had enough. She removed herself from the negative vibes as she often did and marched up to Baxter's office. She waltzed straight in and plopped down in a chair directly across the desk from him.

"Umm, make yourself at home, Katherine."

"Baxter, I don't know what to do, and I need your help. Ron Calais is driving me mad. He doesn't understand the message I'm trying to portray, and he's such a yes-man for this company I don't think he even has a backbone. It's a wonder he can stand up straight!"

Baxter started laughing. "Why don't you tell me what you really think, Katherine?"

She couldn't help but laugh herself. "I'm sorry, but he is ruining my dream. I'm serious," she said, trying to wipe the smile from her face.

"Do you want a new director Katherine?" Baxter's voice was calm and sincere.

"Really? I can have a new director? What will the heads at Fox say?"

"Well, as you know, I have some influence over the heads at Fox, and I know one director they would approve for you. He is more of a producer and has only directed a few independent films, all of which were in a genre completely opposite of yours, but I think he would be perfect for you and this project. Take the rest of the day off, go home, and watch these." Baxter handed her a small pile of DVDs. She agreed and headed home.

Even though it had only been half a day of work, it had been very taxing, and she was grateful to be home. Katherine unlocked the door to her house and poured herself a relaxing drink. Her plan was to sit outside on her patio and bask in the warmth of the afternoon and realign herself with the desired result of the film. But, as she walked out, she saw the DVDs on the table. She picked them up, considered their covers and then walked over to her player and inserted them. She sat back on her sofa and started the first film.

Despite the extreme action and stomach-churning goriness of the films, she could feel that the director was trying to express something deeper than the thrill of the movies. He was hired to direct horror films at this time, which seemed to be about 15 years prior, but they were unlike any scary movie she'd ever seen. Baxter warned her, but he also insisted that she watch each film in its entirety.

It didn't take long before she saw that each film relayed a subtle but powerful message, and she couldn't help but find herself feeling touched at the end. It was something she hadn't seen, even in the best of films. She watched another and another, each empowering her in the most interesting of ways. She called Baxter at three o'clock in the morning, completely oblivious to the time and left a message that James Parker would be their new director.

The next morning Katherine sprang out of bed with renewed vigor. She had been visualizing her first conversation of the day and couldn't wait to get to the set. As she arrived with Baxter by her side she could hear Ron Calais barking orders into the megaphone, creating panic and general stress among the crew. He turned around to see Katherine and Baxter walking toward him.

"I wonder what the witch has got to say to me this morning," he grimaced.

Katherine walked confidently up to him. "Ron, on behalf of myself, the crew, and my executive producer, I have something to say. YOU'RE FIRED!"

Ron looked at her in disbelief, and the crew started cheering.

"I'm sorry, Ron," said Baxter "You're just not right for this project. Come and see me in a minute. I have something else you'll be much better suited to."

While the majority of the crew felt a sense of relief, panic was starting to spread across their faces.

"Don't worry," assured Katherine as she spoke into the megaphone. "We already have a replacement director, and I am confident he will be the right guy to make this movie the way it should be. It's business as usual."

"I'll leave you to it," Baxter said with a cheeky grin on his face.

"What are you grinning about?" asked Katherine.

"Oh nothing. Your new director will be here soon. Call me later, okay?" Baxter walked off in the direction of his office, and Katherine thought she could hear him giggling.

An hour later, her assistant announced that the new director had arrived. Katherine turned in the direction of the car park, as the new director rounded the corner. "What?!"

Glen came strolling around the corner with a cheesy grin plastered all over his face. "What are you doing here?" she asked, clearly confused.

Glen laughed. "Baxter didn't tell you? James Parker is a pseudonym for Glen Peters. I'm your new director."

Go Inside the Chapter:

— Do obstacles and challenges often derail you?

— Do you find that you sometimes have trouble asking for help when you need it?

Scan the code below or go to **www.niywd.com/chp10** to access a free bonus video with author Natalie Ledwell.

Inside, Natalie will reveal how Katherine managed to stay connected to her passion and purpose and moving forward towards her goals in Chapter 10—*despite the you-know-what hitting the fan*—and how you can, too.

You'll also discover Natalie's step-by-step blueprint to becoming unstoppable, so that you can easily blast through any challenges that come your way as you reach for your biggest, most inspiring goals!

CHAPTER ELEVEN

Law of Attraction in Action

Glen had a passion for Katherine that no one in her life had ever had for her. It wasn't until she realized she had it for herself that others came into her life and supported it. He believed in her film and while the studio she chose was already involved, Glen explained to her that he had to take part in some way.

"Darling, I knew I couldn't force myself or my opinions on you. This is your project, and I totally respect that. The thing is, I believe in you and this movie so much, I knew I could make a fantastic contribution. So, I spoke to Baxter, and he agreed that it had to be your choice, your decision. That's why he had the DVDs ready for you to watch, so you could make a decision without pressure or influence from me," Glen explained.

The truth was that he was a director at heart, but he had fallen into producing independent films after his films tanked. He assumed his dream was dead, but it wasn't until he met Katherine that he realized his dream could still live on.

From the very first day, Glen and Katherine were an amazing team together. Their skill set complemented each other perfectly. Because Glen had many years of experience in the industry, he had an innate ability to present Katherine's information in an entertaining and marketable way that still stayed true to her integral message. The love and respect between them permeated through the whole set, and the energy surrounding the entire project was positive, harmonious, and creatively virile.

Katherine created an environment of open collaboration. She was new to the industry and was relying on Glen and the crew to teach her. She encouraged the team to come to her with suggestions, and she always listened with respect and admiration. The crew appreciated her humility and felt like they, too, were making an important contribution to the movie.

There was a noticeable shift in everyone involved with this life-changing project. Watching the message unfold as the project hummed along prompted the crew to approach Katherine so they, too, could improve their lives. And they also wanted to apply these principles to help the success of the film.

Of course, through her own experience, she was able to analyze the success principles she applied on her journey and articulate them in the movie. Actually, teaching people and watching them change, grow, and achieve goals they never thought possible right in front of her eyes was more rewarding than she could have ever imagined.

The first principle she impressed upon them was the importance of starting from a happy place. She recounted the night she adopted her mantra, "I choose to be happy," and how she could feel her vibration rising as she completed her gratitude journal each evening. She remembered the joy she felt when she hit the backspace button, erasing her previous depressing situation and rewriting the happier version of events. She also recalled the night when she first made the connection between being happy and manifesting the successful night in the restaurant playing out exactly the way she visualized.

Katherine knew she would never have set an audacious goal, like creating this movie, if she had been feeling unhappy the way she used to. Before, even when she was feeling okay, she would only set safe, easy-to-attain goals. She only wrote herself out of her current stressful situations and started to dream big once she had mastered a consistent state of happiness.

The crew proved to be quick learners, and it wasn't long before they were sharing with Katherine all the little things they would do to put themselves in a state of happiness. Sitting around the dinner table each night, Joshua, his wife, and children would take turns expressing what they were grateful for that day. Nathan and Amish started volunteering at the local soup kitchen, serving meals to the homeless after work. Caitlin, a production assistant, enrolled in an acting class. It was a secret passion of hers to act, and she loved the new circle of friends she met. Sophie started walking to work, spending an extra 10 minutes meandering through the botanical gardens that were on the way.

Katherine printed out the list of core values Jenny had originally given her so that everyone could identify for themselves who they really were and what values they held higher than anything else in their lives. Bryson shared with Katherine that after completing this exercise, his marriage was better than ever. He explained that when he identified his values in a relationship, he realized that those were the values he loved most about his wife, and he remembered why he fell in love with her. They had both transitioned from focusing on the little things they weren't happy about with each other to focusing on the things they loved and respected about each other. Bryson couldn't thank Katherine enough.

Zac, another crewmember, also confided that he had been approached by a friend who wanted him to start a business on the side, and he had been deliberating over his decision for days. After completing the exercise, it was clear to him that his answer was no. He realized that his friend didn't place the same level of importance on values like discipline, self-control, and loyalty, so becoming business partners would have been disastrous. They decided to remain great friends instead.

Katherine also had the entire team keep a journal to record the limiting, negative thoughts that popped into their minds throughout the day. She then helped them rewrite these thoughts as the positive thoughts they wanted to think. She even spent an afternoon with Clayton, Sebastian, and Grace brainstorming how wealthy, successful people thought about money, how fit, healthy people thought about food and exercise, and how happy people in love thought about their relationships. The four of them filled a whiteboard with these thoughts for the team to add to their individual lists and to benefit from as well.

On the whiteboard, Katherine also added the guidelines for writing affirmations in the most effective way to help elicit clear visualizations that encompassed all aspects of the goals they wanted to achieve and the lives they wanted to live. She also helped those who wanted to create mind movies, so that they had their own movies to watch morning and night.

Language and perception were so important that they had a donation jar in which anyone caught gossiping, passing judgment, saying something unkind, or using the word "can't" had to donate $10. This donation was given to the soup kitchen where Nathan and Amish volunteered. It turned out that Jordan was the biggest contributor to the jar. After a month, the jar was mostly empty. Because Jordan contributed the most, it was his responsibility to personally take the money to the kitchen, where he ended up joining Nathan three evenings a week.

Katherine smiled to herself when she overheard Erynn and Sarah at lunch talking as if they were doing the makeup for the new blockbuster movie *X-Men*, which was scheduled to start a week after the wrap of *Write Here, Write Now*. When she spoke to them about it, they explained how they would finish these discussions with a summary of what they did that day to move closer to their goals. Erynn was attending night classes on special effects makeup and then teaching Sarah what she learned. Sarah made sure she was networking and connecting with anyone who could possibly have anything to do with that movie. Katherine offered to talk to Baxter Barnes for the girls, and their squeals nearly perforated her eardrum.

Katherine recognized that they had created a little ecosystem together where everyone was happy and positive, and, therefore, these states were attracted back to them. Filming was fun and went without a hiccup, which explained why the film was in the can within six months and slightly under budget.

Katherine was happy that the team willingly adopted her teachings and suggestions, even though she was wary about shoving her message down everyone's throat. That being said, there were two things she felt strongly about that she made mandatory. First, everyone had to have 30 minutes of quiet time every day to meditate, pray, visualize their goals, or do whatever they chose to do during that time. This would enable them to unplug from the bustle of the job at hand and reboot so that they could start refreshed and motivated again for the afternoon session. This, she believed, was a key component to the success of the film.

Katherine attributed the success of the film to the fact that every morning and night, every single person who had anything to do with the film, including Baxter Barnes, watched the mind movie that Katherine had created about the film.

The affirmations, photos, and music of this mind movie kept the entire team focused on the success that became more inevitable as the days rolled on. It described how the movie was a worldwide hit, and how it changed the lives of millions. It depicted adoring crowds and raving testimonials. Brittany and Liam were in charge of taking photos of the entire team. Katherine impressed upon the team that no matter what your job was, everyone there played a part in making the movie a success. Each of the photos was included with affirmations detailing the gelling of the team and the individual awards and acclaim they received. It showed records being broken and revenue of $100 million.

The completion of the filming was much like the completion of Katherine's own mind movies. With each scene she wrote for herself, she made sure that it was what she really wanted before she asked for it. With each scene that was filmed for her story, she made sure that it was edited in just the precise format so that it was specific to the message it was telling.

The pressure was intense when the film was submitted to the film festivals. Like any small budget film, the actors and crew wouldn't receive their rewards unless the film did well.

If the film didn't do well, regardless of whether Katherine or anyone would make money, her name would be tarnished in the business, and she would have to work even harder to rebuild it.

Everyone waited impatiently for feedback. Then festivals began accepting the film, and one by one the response was incredible.

∽

The cameras on Renee Carisso's set were rolling, and Katherine's mind reverted back to the present. "Something unexpected happened during the shooting of this film. Something that most people are unaware of," Renee said.

Katherine smiled from ear to ear. Upon a close-up from the camera, it was clear that her cheeks were blushed. "Yes," she affirmed.

"Can you tell us what that was?"

Katherine's behavior went to that of a schoolgirl as she made her announcement. "I became engaged during our shoot." It was the first time anyone had heard of this. Once it was announced it became apparent why Katherine's public appearances were delayed.

"The man you had an impulse to hire as your new director, which to your surprise was Glen, proposed to you just after your first sky-diving experience. Is that correct?" Renee asked.

At the same time, Renee pulled out a picture that would later receive its own close-up in post-production. It was a photo taken of Katherine and Glen, just after the proposal. They stood in an open field with skydiving gear still strapped to them and an exquisite ring to match the exquisite smiles.

"He did." Katherine didn't need to say anymore. The look on her face told the story of love.

"So, not only did you reach the goal of completing the film, but you realized your vision of love at the same time."

Go Inside the Chapter:

— Have you implemented any of the success habits from this book?

— Would you like to get a complete step-by-step system of how each of these success habits fit together?

Scan the code below or go to **www.niywd.com/chp11** to access a free bonus video with author Natalie Ledwell.

Inside, Natalie shares with you a complete play-by-play of how Katherine attracts her perfect partner in Chapter 11, and how you, too, can attract someone who not only meets but far exceeds your expectations.

You'll also receive instant access to a free copy of Natalie's complete success formula for achieving any goal you set for yourself in any area of your life!

CHAPTER TWELVE

So It's Not Just Me

"Did you have any idea the kind of effect this film would have?" Diane Craven continued as they neared the end of that first interview.

"Absolutely. After all, this was my intention." Katherine knew that the film would have this effect on people. She hoped for this grand of a scale, and she believed it, too. The reality of it, though, surpassed her best expectations, which was proving to be a familiar happening in her life.

"In essence, Katherine, the movie that you wrote has been your journey, notwithstanding this moment right now."

"That's right," Katherine said. "As you've now heard about my story and my experience leading up to this point; the film was based on me."

"The film ends with you on a highly-esteemed talk show with an award under your belt. But, you actually have two." She turned to face the crowd, "Audience? Are we inspired?" The audience cheered.

"At times, I'm still pinching myself," Katherine confided. "It was only two short years ago that I was sitting at my table desperately unhappy and helplessly drowning in debt.

Never in my wildest dreams could I have imagined I would be sitting here with you, having accomplished the success of this movie. Even when I did start to visualize and believe I could live the life of my dreams, the life I experience now is so much more than I imagined that if I'd had to struggle for another five years before I got to this place it would have been worth it. The most fulfilling part is that through my movie, people all over the world are learning and applying this knowledge to create their own dream lives."

"We actually have a clip of the movie you made for yourself that kept you in this vibration, thereby allowing you to bring your dreams to fulfillment. It also shows the awards that you earned along the way. This was made before the film went into production. But, before we show it, we'd like to field a few questions from the audience if it's all right with you?" she asked Katherine.

"I would love it," Katherine smiled.

"Let's go right to it," Diane walked into the audience and up to the first gentleman raising his hand.

"Into the mic," Diane directed.

The man, who looked to be in his fifties, cleared his throat, "Um, yes," he paused, a bit nervous. He smiled. "Hi Katherine."

The audience giggled in endearment.

"Hello," she gently replied, sending him relaxed thoughts.

"I appreciate what you have shown us, but can this really happen as you say?" He started to choke up, and his throat sounded like it was closing. "See, my wife was diagnosed with cancer this past year and has since declined in health."

"I'm so sorry," Katherine replied with sincere empathy.

"Thank you. There is hope, and doctors say that she will recover, but it is so hard for us to maintain hope. We've lost our jobs. I had to take so much time off that my boss let me go. My wife's bills are astronomical, and we can't afford our home anymore. It's so hard for us to have good thoughts."

Katherine wiped a tear from her eye. She knew this feeling. "What is your name?"

"Ken."

"Hi Ken. I know how you are feeling. I know how hard it is to find that place of hope when you are inundated with fear and desperation. And, while all of our situations are different, many of us know that feeling." Many people in the audience agreed. "Ken, can you tell me what your number one core value is? The one characteristic that is the truest way to describe yourself?"

Ken took a moment to think and then nodded his head as he affirmed his belief. "Commitment," he said.

Katherine smiled. "Beautiful. And what are the things that you are committed to?"

"Well, my wife and my children. I'm committed to our life together."

"Are you committed to being happy?"

He let his tears flow. "Yes."

"And they are committed to you?"

"Yes." He wiped his eyes.

"Why are you crying right now, Ken?"

"Because I love them so dearly, and I am so grateful to have them. I don't know how we would get through this without each other."

"There you go," Katherine said softly.

Ken stopped crying and asked, "What do you mean?"

"This process will work now that you have reached this point. When was the last time you cried because you were grateful?"

"I can't remember."

"This is the place you need to be. Start from this place. Create your dreams and your goals from this very point of gratitude and watch the changes that take place."

The audience was silent from the emotional interaction.

The microphone was then handed to a well-dressed woman with long blonde hair pulled back into a neat ponytail. "Hi, Katherine," she gushed. "I just want to tell you I am your number one fan." The crowd giggled softly.

"Thank you. What is your question?"

"I was wondering, can you use the Law of Attraction on other people? For example, how can I use it to get my daughter to clean up her room?" The giggling turned into laughter.

"Oh, if only it worked that way!" Katherine laughed. "The only thoughts and actions we can control are our own. Maybe I can help you see a different perspective on this. I can see from the way you present yourself that you value tidiness and cleanliness very highly, and it seems your daughter may not." The woman nodded.

"Well, like I said, you control your own thoughts, so changing the way you look at this will be helpful. Let's say even though your daughter doesn't value tidiness as highly as you, I'm sure she values other things that are positive. How are her school grades?"

"They're really great. She does apply herself to her studies more than I ever did. I do admire her discipline."

"There you go," Katherine said. "If you focus on her positive quality of discipline regarding her studies and other positive qualities, her seeming inability to tidy her room won't bother you so much, and you'll realize that her values are simply different from yours."

"Sure, I could do that. Thank you! You are awesome."
"You're welcome."

"Hello, Katherine," said an attractive woman standing toward the back of the audience. "I think my question is similar to that one."

"No problem, what is your question?" Katherine asked.
"Well, there's this guy I really like."

"Yes, I think I know where this question is heading." The audience laughed.

"Well, we are perfect for each other, and we have a great time when we're together. It's just that we've been seeing each other for a year on and off, and it doesn't seem to be going anywhere. How can I use Law of Attraction to make him realize we should be together?"

"Honey, what is your name?"

"Marie."

"Okay, Marie, I just want you to know that you're not alone in this situation, but you are making a very common mistake. You see, by focusing on one particular guy you are assuming the job of the universe. You think that this guy is how you will get the relationship you want, but that's not up to you. When you get home today, grab yourself a nice glass of wine, some paper and a pen and write a list of affirmations that describes the characteristics of your perfect guy. Describe the relationship you want, the things you do together. Describe what life looks like with the perfect relationship and the characteristics you need to have in order to attract this perfect guy. Then write action affirmations describing what you need to do to meet this guy. You will be better served focusing on this list rather than one particular person who, I have to say, would be with you if that were what he really wanted. Stop wasting time here and be proactive about meeting the guy you deserve." The crowd erupted with applause.

"We have time for one more question before we cut to commercial," Diane announced. "Yes, over there in the blue shirt."

A guy stood up and nervously took the microphone.

"Umm, yeah, I'm wondering if this stuff works if you don't really believe in it?" the crowd looked intently back to Katherine.

"Great question. When we talk about the LOA, we are talking about a universal law that has always existed. Let me ask you this. Does gravity still work whether you believe in it or not?"

"I guess so."

"The same applies to the Law of Attraction. For me, the revelation was realizing that it existed and then figuring out how it worked. Once I did this, I started making different choices, thinking different thoughts, and taking different actions, so I could positively change the outcomes in my life. The Law of Attraction explains why this happens, which builds my belief that it works every time. My suggestion is to start with small things to build your faith, and then move onto monumental things that not only positively affect you but those around you as well."

Diane cut to a commercial.

After a few more questions and praises, Diane asked, "Can we show it?"

The audience went wild. To see the original mind movie that Katherine made to get her to this point exceeded their expectations. Katherine nodded.

Diane faced the camera. "Take a look."

The lights in the studio lowered as the screen behind Diane and Katherine opened on the mind movie that showed the pictures of fingers typing away, a film being accepted and made, and thousands of people being empowered by the film. The affirmations floated on and off the screen as music played, showing image after image of Katherine's intention and desire. The audience seemed to be lost in her creation and absorbing the emotions it invoked.

When the short movie came to an end, the audience stayed silent as they realized that they had just witnessed how this all came to be.

After a few moments of silence, Diane chimed in, "In fact, Katherine, this movie you made is quite accurate. Just look at the effect *Write Here, Write Now* has had." She directed her attention again at the screen as pictures of letters and emails from people were shown. Pieces of the letters were highlighted, showing the most poignant effect it had on these people's lives. As one image flew out, another flew in. The words expanded so that everyone could read about how these people were encouraged as a result of Katherine's film.

The quotes continued to roll in and out proclaiming, "Katherine's movie has forever changed my life." Another showed an image of a heavyset man, with the now thin and healthy version of himself standing in front of the picture. "I watched *Write Here, Write Now*, and I made my first movie that same night. Three months later, I am healthier than I have ever been in my life," he said.

Another photo popped onto the screen of a woman and an older man. "I found my father after 19 years because of Katherine's film," the woman said. "I knew he was out there."

"I was a divorced, single mom of twin babies. I'd lost everything I had. I had no idea what I was capable of until I saw this film," another woman added. "I just bought my first house and landed an executive position. I've never been happier. Thank you, Katherine."

Music continued to play as more and more quotes and stories were seen and heard. Couples getting married, businesses growing exponentially, men and woman regaining their health, illnesses vanishing, and dreams coming true.

As the medley of compliments and gratitude faded and the screen turned to black again, Diane held the silence and declared the moment they'd all been waiting for, when they could speak to Katherine. "We'll be right back."

The cameras stopped rolling and Katherine was brimming with emotion. Tears delicately dropped onto her cheekbone. Diane set her hand on Katherine's knee. "You did it, and it's only the beginning." Glen, her family, and her friends were sitting in the front row, beaming and proud.

A month and a half later, Katherine sat next to her fiancé, Glen, in the first-class section of a plane. They were on their way to celebrate the success of the film, the completion of the press tour, and to get married on a tropical island. Life was bigger than she ever dreamed possible. Now that she knew this was possible, there was nothing that she couldn't do.

Glen leaned in to kiss her softly on the cheek. A rush of love went through her body. "You know," he said. "I have to say. People love watching you on all of those shows. It's like you are speaking directly to them. Imagine if you had your own show? Imagine how many lives you could change?"

Katherine turned her head to him immediately. "I think I have my next project."

Go Inside the Chapter:

— Is there one particular lesson in this book that struck a cord with you over the others? Are you hungry for more?

— Are you ready to finally break out of what's not working for you in your life and open yourself up to all of the happiness, passion and purpose you deserve and desire?

Scan the code below or go to **www.niywd.com/chp12** to access a free bonus video with author Natalie Ledwell.

Inside, Natalie reveals how Katherine integrates everything she's learned throughout her journey, allowing her to live life with more effortless ease, flow and abundance—*and how you can follow in her footsteps.*

Plus, you'll discover how you can mastermind with Natalie and a unique, amazing dream team of people from all over the world, all striving to hit their goals and create lives they love just like you!

The End

ABOUT THE AUTHOR

Natalie Ledwell is a Law of Attraction evangelist. She has positively impacted the lives of millions of people around the world by empowering them to achieve their dreams by first knowing what they want then creating a personal "digital" vision board or Mind Movie to invoke the principles of The Law of Attraction. She grew up in Orange NSW, Australia, number five in a family of eight children. At the age of 18 she left her family, friends and everything she knew and moved to Sydney to pursue a career in Fitness. It was at the age of 21 she realized it was possible to achieve anything she set her mind to when was introduced to Personal Development motivational information in the form of a set of Brian Tracey cassette's her boss lent to her. In 1995 she met her husband Glen and they embarked on a 10 year serial entrepreneurship owning and operating along list of businesses. Years of seminars, books, goal setting, weekend retreats, hot coal walking combined with hard work and just about every type of business under the sun, left her feeling frustrated, helpless and questioning what else could she do to live the life she always dreamed of. In 2006 Natalie experienced a life changing epiphany when she watched a movie called

The Secret. This lead her down an inspired path of Law of Attraction research and application. Now Natalie gratefully lives a life beyond her wildest dreams. She lives an endless summer, travels the world,and has an incredible circle of friend who share her positive mindset and provides amazing support. She calls her mentors Bob Proctor, John Assaraf, Bob Doyle and Joe Vitale, friends. In 4 short years Natalie along with her husband Glen and business partner Ryan Higgins built a multimillion dollar online business and are grateful that through this business they are making a positive impact throughout the world. Natalie's passion is to help as many people as possible realize they can live the life of their dreams through this book, her live presentations, her online TV show www.theinspirationshow.com and life enhancing resources available through www.mindmovies.com.